PREPARING FOR CHURCH MINISTRY

A PRACTICAL GUIDE TO SPIRITUAL FORMATION

by

ALFRED CLIFTON HUGHES

Foreword by Adrian van Kaam, C.S.Sp.

DIMENSION BOOKS

Denville, New Jersey 07834

DEDICATION

To my Mother and Father
who under God were the first
to form me for life and Church ministry
and to all who have revealed
God's saving presence to me.

First English Edition by Dimension Books

Denville, New Jersey 07834

Copyright © 1979 by Alfred Clifton Hughes

TABLE OF CONTENTS

PART TWO

Acknowledgements

The author acknowledges with great gratitude the kindness of Humberto Cardinal Medeiros, the fraternal support of the faculty of St. John's Seminary, the grace of exercising a formational ministry with St. John's Spiritual Direction Staff, the wisdom and encouragement of Rev. Adrian van Kaam and the staff of the Institute of Formative Spirituality at Duquesne University, the perceptive counsel shared with me by Rev. Msgr. Joseph Moody, Rev. Robert Banks and Rev. Mark Noonan after their careful reading of my first manuscript, the official assurance of Rev. Msgr. Matthew Stapleton that the content of this book is consonant with faith and doctrine, the Christian hospitality of the monks of St. Anselm's Abbey in Manchester during the weeks of writing, the painstaking, generous labor of Sister Dorothy Welch, C.S.J. who typed the entire text as an expression of her desire to serve God's word and finally the trust of so many lay, religious and ordained who have shared the sacred intimacy of their own spiritual journey in personal spiritual direction. May the work of this writer not betray either the Word of God or the confidence and generosity of these good people.

The author is pleased to acknowledge with thanks the following permissions. If any acknowledgements have inadvertently been omitted, this will be rectified in a future edition.

Scriptural quotations are taken from *The Jerusalem Bible,* copyright © 1966 by Darton, Longman and Todd, Ltd. and Doubleday and Company, Inc. Used by permission of the publisher.

Quotations from *A Man For All Seasons,* copyright © 1960, 1962 by Robert Bolt, are included with permission of the publisher, Random House, Inc., Alfred A. Knopp, Inc.

Quotations from *The Power and the Glory,* copyright © 1940 by Graham Greene, are included with permission of the publisher, Viking Press.

FOREWORD

By Adrian van Kaam, C.S.Sp.

This wise and balanced book by Father Hughes is a genuine guide to spiritual formation in preparation for Church ministry.

The author makes clear that spiritual formation is not a process of molding the future minister from the outside. Rather it is a life-long attempt to disclose and unfold the life form God has meant for each minister in great personal care and love. The fundamental question is: how can we remove obstacles and create with God's grace conditions that facilitate the disclosure and implementation of the life form we are called to in Jesus? To answer this question the author goes deeply into the signs that help us recognize whether or not we are called to one of the many ministries emerging in the Church today. He points out what kind of formation such ministry entails.

Reading his appraisal of right spiritual formation we feel grateful that Christ became man to assist our transformation into him and through him into the divine form God has meant for us from eternity. St. Paul tells us that Jesus will transform these wretched bodies of ours into forms of his glorious body (Ph. 3:21). The author helps us to see that such transformation presupposes that we are honest with ourselves, take off our masks, unveil our make-believe faces, and then "we, with our unveiled faces will reflect like mirrors the brightness of the Lord, all grow brighter . . . as we are transformed into the form that we reflect" (2 Cor. 3:18).

Such formation in the estimation of Father Hughes is especially important for those who are called not only to find their own life form in Christ, but also to minister to others searching for their form in Him. Ministry is suffering for the formation of others. "I must go through the pain of giving birth to you all over again, until Christ is formed in you" (Gal. 4:19). "Take me for your form as I take Christ" (1 Cor. 11:1). "Never be a dictator of any group that is put in your charge, but be a form that the whole flock can follow" (1 Pet. 5:3).

The need for grace and sacrament runs as a golden thread through the whole book. No spiritual formation for ministry can succeed without this personal continuous assistance of the Lord. How true this is. For God alone is the mysterious inexhaustible origin of all forms emerging and re-emerging in his creation. His human creatures too are not autonomous "self actualizers." We are called to be with Him co-originators of our ministerial form of life. He originated in the depths of our being his image. To be sure, no minister of the Church can carry in himself and in his ministry the total image of the infinite God. Each minister is called to reflect in a limited and unique way the mystery of the Divine. In that sense we are all originals in our shared and common ministry. It takes, however, a life time of co-origination with grace to be formed into the original yet common way of ministry God has meant for us from eternity.

Father Hughes makes us deeply aware of this life long task of ministerial self formation in and through a truly ecclesiastical spirituality. A minister of the Church should be formed in and through the Church. Ecclesiastical prayer is stressed and rightly so. Our deepest ministerial self is a living relationship with God, together with the Church, the people of God we are called to serve in a special way. The eternal Father originates us as Church together in Jesus. The more we become in and through the Church the ministers the Lord lovingly calls us to be, the more we will be one with our divine Origin. This union with the mystery of our most holy Origin deepens the formative power of our ministry.

This sound and thoughtful book by an outstanding spiritual teacher and director solves many confusions about ministry and spiritual formation. It enlightens and inspires us by its wisdom and its faith. We hope that many men and women preparing themselves for one of the many ministries emerging in the Church today may gratefully assimilate the wisdom and experience contained within these pages.

INTRODUCTION

SHARING CHURCH MINISTRY

The Church has been alive in the present decade with a debate over ministry—team ministry, lay ministry, special ministry, shared ministry. Perhaps the Holy Spirit has stirred up ferment in the church in general and priestly ministry in particular to awaken all of us to the rich possibilities of varied services which have remained dormant in the Church in recent years.

Men and women, young and old are stepping forward in search of officially recognized Church ministries. Despite the fact that fewer knock at the doors of diocesan seminaries or the novitiates of apostolic religious communities, many are volunteering as lectors and extraordinary ministers of the Eucharist, a significant number have presented themselves as applicants for the permanent diaconate and numerous women, especially religious women, are exploring the possibilities of larger ministerial responsibilities in the church, including ordination to diaconate and priesthood.

Some young people are innovative in experimenting with interdisciplinary ways to prepare for possible future ministries. Creative individuals have pioneered new approaches in hospital, prison, and parish ministry. Some have explored the possibilities of a more explicitly spiritual ministry in connection with one of the current spiritual movements or with a center for prayer and spiritual guidance. Socially-committed persons have labored hard to awaken the Church and local governments to the cries of the poor and the oppressed. Every minority group has looked for representation in the leadership of the Church.

In the midst of this ferment, some prominent Chicago leaders have issued a "Declaration of Concern: On Devaluing the Laity."[1] They strongly support the Second Vatican Council's Decree on the Laity (*Apostolicam Actuositatem*), but openly lament the present post-conciliar tendency to absorb gifted Christian lay persons into an *explicit* Church ministry. Is this obscuring the more central apostolate of lay people which is to reach out redemptively to family, to work and to society?

Priests' senates, sisters' senates, diocesan councils, organizations promoting new approaches to ministry and the Detroit Call to Action have entered into extensive consultation, conducted symposia and formulated proposals. As the Spirit leads us into a promising future, we are called not only to discern the signs of the times beckoning us to con-

[1]*Origins,* Vol. 7 (1977-1978), pp. 440-442.

sider new ministerial possibilities, but also to discern which possibilities truly come from the Holy Spirit.

In pondering these developments, some realities strike me very forcibly: first, there are many rich gifts in the church which need to be recognized and encouraged; secondly, there is a need to clarify better the different, yet complementary roles in the Church; thirdly, individuals need more help in discerning their true vocations; lastly, the Church will want to offer sound spiritual formation to all those who enter a Church ministry. Let me develop each of these briefly and then indicate the purpose of this book.

A variety of gifts for ministry

In the recent past, preparation for Church ministry has generally deemphasized creativity. The embrace of discipline and the fulfillment of prescribed tasks have been regarded as more important. But in our present culture, we are educated to explore, experiment and innovate. Hence young adults are much more conscious of unique talents, training and opportunities which they would like to actualize. Some would like to offer these to the Church.

Moreover, the media help us to become more aware of the great needs of other people, both near and far. We know the poverty of the dispossessed, the hunger of famine-stricken areas, the injustice inflicted by racial, ethnic, religious or gender bias, the ravages of war, the suppression of human rights, the wounds inflicted by so much crime and violence, the loss of respect for fragile human life, the plight of prisoners. These needs in society cry out for constructive and creative action. Many look to the Church for leadership and guidance.

In addition, we hear of personal anguish. Relatives, friends and neighbors suffer physically, emotionally or financially in ways that cry out for compassion and assistance. Fear, loneliness and alienation seem to engulf so many. These persons, too, will often turn to the Church for solace, understanding, and help.

Many young people desire to contribute. They want to reach out to those who suffer. They often want to serve in the name of Jesus Christ and his Church. They are pained when the possibilities are too limited.

One mission: different and complementary roles

Before rushing to the conclusion that the Church ought to seize the present opportunity and sponsor every new venture in ministry, it may be helpful to clarify an important distinction between Church *mission* and Church *ministry*. The mission is global; ministry is more limited.

Like the mission of Jesus himself, the Church's mission is to save and renew every creature. The Church has the broad mandate: "that by spreading the kingdom of Christ everywhere for the glory of God the Father, she might bring all men to share in Christ's saving redemption; and that through them the whole world might in actual fact be brought into relationship with him" (*Apostolicam Actuositatem,* 2). This mission belongs to the *whole* church. By baptism and confirmation, all of us are incorporated into Christ's life and expected to join with him in his redemptive love for the world. Christ desires that every area of human life be touched by his saving grace. "The joys and the hopes, the griefs and the anxieties of the men of this age, especially those who are poor or in any way afflicted, these too are the joys and hopes, the griefs and anxieties of the followers of Christ. Indeed, nothing genuinely human fails to raise an echo in their hearts" (*Gaudium et Spes,*).

However universal and all-encompassing is the Church's mission, ministry in the Church depends on a particular vocation in the Church. Ministries, then, flow from the common mission which all in the Church share, but no one ministry is identical with the entire mission of the Church. There is a sense in which each of our vocations is unique and, therefore, ministry in life is also unique. But it is also possible to speak in more general terms of a ministry that belongs to the laity in the Church and another ministry which belongs to the ordained. Both share in the Church's universal mission, but in accordance with the sacramental life in which each shares.

The laity "exercise a genuine apostolate by their activity on behalf of penetrating and perfecting the temporal sphere of things through the spirit of the gospel" (*Apostolicam Actuositatem,* 2). Their first responsibility, then, is to incarnate the gospel in their lives in such a way that they make the life of Christ attractive to others. The most effective preaching is the gospel enfleshed in life. It invites others to want to explore the mystery which animates such life. It sanctifies the lives of those around. In addition to the evangelizing and sanctifying roles that the laity are urged to embrace in the way they live their lives, they also have a special responsibility to bring their faith and ethical witness to those areas of life which their vocation and work call them to influence. Thus, they have a special role in contributing to the sanctification of marriage, family life, secular fields of employment and society as a whole. Twentieth-century life has become quite complex. Many areas of human life have come to develop a secular autonomy. Lay persons deeply involved in these sectors of life are in the best position to bring the transforming power of the gospel to them.

The ordained in the Church have a more specific ministry. "With their helpers, the priests and deacons, bishops have therefore taken up the service of the community, presiding in place of God over the flock whose shepherds they are, as teachers of doctrine, priests of sacred worship and officers of good order" (*Lumen Gentium,* 20). In their lives, the more general ministry of the whole People of God is given a further specification. Like the laity, they, too, are called to live the Christian life in such a way that they reveal the power of the gospel and attract others to holiness of life. But instead of a mandate to become directly involved in transforming the secular order, they are commissioned to preach God's word, teach its fuller meaning, offer prayer and sacramental worship and bring holy order to the household of God. These responsibilities are not arbitrarily assumed by them. They flow from the nature of the sacrament of order. By virtue of orders, men are permanently incorporated into Christ's role of head of his body, the Church. Hence, they exercise his prophetical, priestly and ruling ministry in his name.

The religious who may be either ordained or lay members of the Church "imitate Christ the virgin and the poor man (cf. Mt. 8:20; Lk. 9:58), who by an obedience which carried him even to death on the cross (cf. Phil. 2:8), redeemed men and made them holy. As a consequence, impelled by a love which the Holy Spirit has poured into their hearts (cf.Rm.5:5), these Christians spend themselves ever increasingly for Christ, and for his body the Church (cf. Col.1:24)" (*Perfectae caritatis,*). Religious are not an intermediate step between orders and lay life. Rather, the faithful are called by God from *both* states of life to further the mission of the church (cf. *Lumen gentium,* 43). Religious have a special role of being a sign to both the ordained and the laity of the call God gives all in Christ Jesus to holiness of life in the Holy Spirit. All the People of God are called and empowered to become holy (cf. *Lumen gentium,* 39-42). But religious who live publicly consecrated lives are *signs* of this universal call (*Lumen gentium,* 44).

The biblical image which seems most helpful in sketching an outline for collaboration in the Church is the body of Christ (1 Cor. 12:4-30). Thus, all the people in the Church are parts of Christ's body: the laity, as *members* of the body, have the role of extending Christ's redemptive mission throughout family, professional and occupational life and society at large; the ordained, as the *visible head* of the body, have the role of making concrete on the local scene the preaching, worshipping and guiding role of Christ himself; the religious, as the *heart* of the body, have the role of being a tangible sign of Christ's call to consecrated love.

In practice, the roles are not that simply demarcated. There should be a mutual interplay among them. The laity, beyond fulfilling their own roles, may help the ordained to relate preaching to the real issues in the lives of people or to expand pastoral care to pressing concerns in society, may cooperate in explicit Church ministry and may offer the example of extraordinary holiness of life. The ordained, beyond fulfilling their own roles, will be challenged by the religious to live their own central call to holiness of life and will be invited by lay persons to recognize that the Church's mission reaches far beyond ecclesiastical concerns to the ordinary issues of daily life and the social, economic, and political conditions in society. The religious, beyond fulfilling their own role in being a special sign of holiness, may share in some aspects of explicit Church ministry (pastoral out-reach, spiritual guidance, catechesis) or may be involved in some of the more usual lay tasks (teaching, nursing care, domestic service, social service, involvement in social change.)

As an underlying model for collaboration, the biblical image of Christ's body helps us appreciate the need for both unity and diversity. This model is not secular, competitive or univocal, but sacramental, collaborative and complementary. It is rooted in the deeper shared life and mission of Jesus Christ.

Discernment of vocation for Church Ministry

Understanding, then, the difference between the Church's universal mission and the particular ministries of its members and recognizing that the laity, ordained and religious are called to different, yet complementary roles in the church, can we clarify the meaning of *Church Ministry?* Church ministry is the ministry of word, sacrament and pastoral guidance which belongs properly to the ordained bishops, priests and deacons, but which may also be shared in an explicit, yet analogous way by laity and religious.

Church ministry does not include the broad and varied ventures which are the province of the laity as they reach into every sector of human existence. This is why Church documents normally do not use the term *ministry* for the laity, but speak instead of the lay apostolate. The use of the term, lay apostolate, does not connote second-class importance for the work of the laity. Rather it draws attention to the distinctiveness of this task. The lay apostolate, generously embraced, has traditionally been the most fruitful way to christianize the environment and the culture. In many ways the vitality of the Church in any era can be best measured by the extent of lay participation in the Christianizing of the environment. Many would argue rather persuasively that the more pressing need today is to help the laity to appreciate the autonomous and critical role they play in transforming society.

The purpose of this book is limited. My concern will be principally to reach out to those who seek to enter the Church ministry of word, sacrament and pastoral guidance. The numbers approaching sacramental ordination are small. But there is a growing number of laity and religious who wish to associate themselves with the ordained ministry in a real, although distinct way. Often they do not know clearly what they seek. They are aware of a vague desire to be explicitly associated with church ministry and to serve others. They are not sure whether the ordained will understand them or allow them a participative role. They usually want to resist clericalization. They wonder about financing such a life. They often look in vain for assistance.

I would like to suggest that one of the important ways to prepare for Church ministry is to discern the vocation with care in the context of genuine spiritual formation. An initial desire may be very superficial and come from unhealthy needs or it may come from the depths of the heart graced by the Holy Spirit. The desire, then, needs to be tested with the Church so that it becomes more possible to determine what is truly of God and what is not.

It is sad to see well-intentioned men and women consume a tremendous amount of time, energy and finances in preparing for a ministerial role which they then are not able to enter. This may be due to factors within themselves: a basic unsuitability, a crippling immaturity, serious moral weakness or spiritual superficiality. Or this may be due to the fact that the local ordained Church leaders have not yet incorporated a particular expression of ministry into the official Church ministry. When disappointment comes, the hurt can lead to great anger. And festering resentment may close off much of any further spiritual growth or possibility for fruitful service for the kingdom of God. Sometimes, these individuals will be tempted to spite the Church by volunteering for ministry in a less sacramentally-rooted Christian tradition or by entering into bitterly hostile behavior against the Church. A responsible and realistic discernment of vocation within a program of sound spiritual formation can help to minimize these heart-rendering situations.

We can gain a further insight into the importance of this discernment by drawing on the conclusions of research done with religious and priests in recent years by Luigi Rulla, Joyce Ridick and Francis Imoda.[2] Over a period of ten years since the Second Vatican Council, they followed the development of over six hundred candidates for religious life and priesthood. They concluded that an extremely important factor in departure from religious vocation has been the subsequent loneliness and alienation experienced by those who never were able to accept *internally* the transcendent values in their vocation. The researchers suggest that perceptive formation personnel might have helped some such candidates recognize and deal with the real discrepancies or inconsistencies between the inner values actually operative in them and the objective values which they were claiming to espouse in a transcendent religious vocation, such as: the experience and love of God, the desire to imitate Jesus Christ, the attraction to a greater life of evangelical poverty, celibate love and obedience in the way expected by priesthood or a religious institute.

Formation personnel, in recognizing problematic patterns and even making some hard decisions during the training period, can save many a heartache later on.

[2]Rulla, *et al, Entering and Leaving Religious Vocation: Intrapsychic Dynamics* (Rome: Gregorian University Press and Chicago: Loyola University Press, 1976).

It is possible to learn from this research. For example, candidates who experience a long-standing inability to sustain any personal prayer, may find with help that this is due less to failures in self-discipline and more to an instinctive fear or anger when approaching God. If candidates experience difficulty in entering into self-revelation in a spiritual direction relationship, they may discover that this is due less to shyness and more to an inability to entrust inner conflict and confusion to a trusted father. Candidates may learn that their hyperactive involvement in serving the needs of others may be less expressive of Christian zeal and reveal more a deeper disquietude of spirit. To enter into this kind of self-knowledge, any human being needs competent help.

Toward sound spiritual formation

As we explore the possibilities of the present moment in Church history, it becomes clearer that the sound spiritual maturation of potential church ministries is extremely central. The role of the Church is not just to multiply service to others. It is to further the redemptive mission of Jesus Christ. If the explicit Church ministry can be exercised in such a way that all the members of the Church become more aware of their unique call to contribute to Christ's redemptive work in the world, then many varied services will develop apart from explicit Church sponsorship.

This understanding of Church ministry means that those who enter it must have grown in sufficient depth in faith and moral living to be able to help others do the same. They must be moving into greater communion with God, a deeper conversion of heart, a more expansive charity and a more mature love for the Church. This gradual inner transformation should lead to a greater consecration of their sexual love, detachment of spirit, cooperation with sacramental authority, sharing in ecclesial prayer and progress in pastoral charity. It is spiritual maturity that draws others to maturity in their lives. It is holiness that attracts others to a holy way of life.

This book, then, is written in an atmosphere of creative ferment in Church ministry, at a time when there is some confusion over distinctive roles in the Church, in a situation where discernment of vocation is not easy and sound spiritual formation is a pressing need. The book is an attempt to express what is central to spiritual formation for Church ministry in the Catholic tradition. It is addressed to all who wish to explore the possibility of depth in Church ministry.

The book is divided into two parts. The first part treats of those fundamental realities which undergird any authentic decision to seek Church ministry. This section should also have significant relevance for any Christian who wishes to lead a richer spiritual life. The second part addresses the significant factors for growth in depth in church ministry.

This section should also be helpful to those who already have entered Church ministry. A final chapter offers some more specific comments for those who are engaged in the challenging role of preparing others for Church ministry.

Although Church ministry has in the recent past been composed almost exclusively of the ordained, this book is addressed not only to those who are entering ordained ministry—the diaconate, priesthood or episcopate; but also to those who aspire to an officially endorsed Church ministry—the pastoral ministry of religious and lay persons in parishes, spiritual and social centers, prisons and hospitals. Although there are factors which are obviously unique to the spirituality of each group, there is also a common ecclesial ministerial spirituality which preceeds and underlies their more specific vocational calls. The author hopes to suggest what constitutes a core ecclesial spiritual formation. Suggestions for more particular applications to the laity, the ordained or the religious are made wherever such remarks seem appropriate.

These reflections are offered for meditative reading. It is my hope that they may assist some few to hear more attentively and to answer more generously Christ's probing invitation: "What are you looking for?" (Jn. 1:38)

PART I

THE ROAD TO DECISION FOR CHURCH MINISTRY

The desire for church ministry is like a seed. It may be a good seed; it may be a potential weed. But at the beginning, it is often difficult to tell the difference. Rather than focus all our attention on trying to determine at the outset which it is, there is usually more merit in tilling the soil, removing any rocks and providing sufficient moisture and fertilizer. The true nature of the doubtful seed will become gradually more obvious.

Part I of this book is about tilling the soil, removing the obstacles and providing adequate nourishment so that we can discern better the difference between seed sown by God and seed that is sown by an enemy (cf. Mt. 13:25). It is addressed to all who want to live a deeper Christian spiritual life, but in a special way to those who think they may have a special calling to enter Church ministry.

GROWING COMMUNION WITH GOD

Our scientific and technological culture provides us with extraordinary possibilities in our struggle to meet the challenges of this world. This same scientifically sophisticated culture tends, at times, to lay a heavy burden on us. A hundred years ago, as the industrial age was first emerging, Charles Dickens perceptively recognized the mixed blessings of scientific progress. His novel, *Hard Times,* begins: "Now, what I want is, Facts. Teach these boys and girls nothing but Facts. Facts alone are wanted in life. Plant nothing else, and root out everything else. You can only form the minds of reasoning animals upon Facts; nothing else will ever be of service to them."[1] These are the spiritless words of Thomas Gradgrind, owner and policy-maker for the local school, himself the product of a strictly scientific education. His insistence on this extreme educational policy left no room for wonder, imagination, the emotional or spiritual life. Dickens appropriately entitled the following chapter: "Murdering the Innocents." And then he proceeded to unveil the dramatic human struggle through which various participants in this educational experiment had to pass in order to discover the transcendent in life.

The need for transcendence

The phenomenon which Dickens described in the last century has continued into our own era. The more industrialized the area, the more daily life seems to be controlled by machines and the scientific mentality. Obviously machines and scientific developments can free us from much debilitating labor; they can also enslave and dehumanize us. The young sometimes seem particularly sensitive to this dilemma as they find themselves torn between craving the attractive products of a highly mechanized society on the one hand, and wanting, on the other, an idyllic existence free of the competitive and enervating pressures of this complex society. They rightly sense a problem, even if they do not yet phrase the question correctly.

Another example of this is the pervasive feeling of powerlessness which many of us experience in our cities. We may feel hemmed in by the economic and social forces beyond our control. Modern life sometimes seems too complicated and oppressive. In a certain sense,

---

[1]Charles Dickens, *HARD TIMES,* George Ford and Sylvere Monod, ed. (New York: W.W. Norton & Co., 1966), p. 1.

pollution seems to have become a symbol of this suffocating existence. Instead of nature being friendly and uplifting to the human spirit, people experience air pollution, water pollution and noise pollution. Instead of *human* nature being inspiring and supportive of deeper life, we struggle with porno pollution, mind pollution and spiritual pollution.

We cannot become obscurantist. There is so much in developing science, technology and cybernetics which serves us and frees us for richer living. It is no service to Christian spirituality to denigrate authentic human progress. What we do want is to become free of *polluting* patterns of life. There are innumerable fascinating and captivating sights, sounds, smells, tastes and touches. Can we also see, hear, smell, taste and touch the *fascinans tremendum?* The great yearning of the human heart is for expansiveness of spirit, truth, beauty and real love. One of the most fundamental choices we make in life is between a life lived in open and friendly dialogue with a self-transcendent Reality or a life restricted by the seductive, restrictive horizons of purely secular reality. The human choice involved here touches the roots of our being. We can find it frightening. For we experience the call to reach beyond the self as both enticing and risky. It always involves some separation from people and a way of life which have been familiar and trusted. It implies detachment. It leads to a new life, but only at the price of a real death.

Ordinarily it is not possible to sustain this movement toward self-transcendent life without support and direction from others who are more experienced. It is not always easy to find good direction. The Church does try to offer more personal direction for those who are going to enter into a more public Church ministry for others. But where this is lacking, the wisdom of the spiritual masters as preserved for us in the Christian spiritual classics offers us the most reliable guidance in this endeavor.

Spiritual masters of every epoch have focused on the centrality of this struggle. With firmness and persistence they invite us to face courageously the required transformation. Many people do not understand this emphasis on transcendence. Voices around us may urge us to enter into busy daily schedules, intense academic study, extensive pastoral experience, broader social involvement. Those concerns have their rightful place. But the initial step in movement into deeper life involves a quieting of the heart and a weaning of ourselves away from hectic activity.

Fidelity to this movement comes hard. It usually involves a real grieving over the loss of our previous way of life. We may have come to associate being alive with hyperactivity. The attractions without and the initial discomfort within can shatter fragile self-confidence. The temptation is either to give up the struggle altogether or to substitute some good and noble cause for the transcendent God.

In the last decade there has been no lack of exciting causes to seize the imagination and fan the flames of enthusiasm in good people. We have lived through a series of different emphases in spirituality: a renewed appreciation of the bible, the reformation of the Church's liturgy, the opening of the Church to the world, concern for the inner city and the poor, increased awareness of the need for ecumenical collaboration, involvement in the struggle to eradicate racism, immersion in the darkness of the death-of-God movement, mobilization of the forces of war-resistance, involvement in the theology of hope, experimentation with eastern approaches to prayer, enthusiastic participation in the charismatic renewal or the various encounter movements, concern over the role of women in society and the church. Obviously, these movements touch profound Christian concerns. Each can easily capture the imagination and touch the human heart which craves most of all to give itself over to a life bigger than its own. Religious leaders, theologians, even formation directors can be easily seduced into substituting a noble cause for the transcendent God. So, keeping the proper focus requires a great deal of us. We want to beg God's grace to move our hearts beyond even the most noble of human ideals so that we may be touched and grasped by the God who effects a transformation reaching into every area of our life.

Initiation into transcendence

Awakening ourselves to our great need for transcendent experience is only a beginning. We want to discover ways to uncover our desire and foster our experience of mystery. Perhaps a good place to begin is with our approach to leisure time.

Have you ever reflected on the meaning of a sabbath or a vacation? Is it just time off from regular work? Is it merely human compensation for the accomplishment of a relentless series of tasks?

"Remember the sabbath day and keep it holy" (Ex.20:8). The Judaeo-Christian spiritual tradition associates the sabbath with the holy, the transcendent. The faithful have been urged over the centuries to set aside the managerial function in life in order to dwell with the God who creates, supports and redeems life. It is a time for leisure, relaxing hobbies, play, inspiring reading, prayer and public worship.

The Puritans had a sound insight into the sacredness of the whole day. But they approached the day in the wrong way. Instead of its being a day that touched the spirit and lifted the heart, it became a day of sober moralisms which carefully regimented behavior and laid heavier burdens on the people. It is no wonder that this oppressive atmosphere later triggered a revolt by the Unitarians who recognized that God is more transcendent and by the philosophical transcendentalists who were so much in tune with nature.

A Practical Guide To Spiritual Formation

Regretfully, the current wave of economic pragmatism seems to be systematically sweeping away every civil ordinance which in some way fostered a sabbath experience. This is robbing society of social support for transcendent life. The demanding pace of our own culture is taking its toll. Even those who are able to conquer its challenges and reach the top seem to encounter a depressing uneasiness and a sense of emptiness within. The repressed spirit can nudge people into tragic self-destruction through alcohol or drug abuse, promiscuous sexual activity, serial marriages, frantic experimentation with new careers and even suicide itself. It is one of the ironies of this scientifically-sophisticated age that so many people have returned to various expressions of the occult and even devil worship to handle their anxieties and fears about an alien spirit world.

We need a sabbath-like experience to foster inner quiet and a consciousness of deeper mystery. It is no surprise, then, that more and more people are exploring ways to slow themselves down and to find an inner calm. Some turn to the east for zen Buddhist or Hindu yoga techniques. Some turn to the Moslem or eastern Christian practice of repetitive prayer. Some turn to recently developed mind control or centering practices. The anxiety engendered by the suppressed spirit leaves people very uneasy.

We, too, have come from this culture. Sometimes, when we take the time to slow down and pause, we find that greater difficulties lie within ourselves. For instance, we probably enjoy a more sophisticated educational background and more inquisitive minds than many people who have gone before us. We have learned to experiment and create and analyze. Even though not fully matured and experiencing considerable self-doubt within, we may often try to approach life in a very self-assured way. Advanced education usually sharpens the intellect and refines a person's capacity to understand and criticize. This is an extremely helpful resource for living and working in today's world. The experience of learning and understanding is one of mastery. It provides a sense of power and control over hitherto mysterious and, therefore, threatening realities. It builds confidence and the courage to walk in the company of accomplished people. Yet there is something more, something which cannot be so grasped. In fact, in order to begin to touch it, it is necessary to let go of the grasping mentality. A person has to be grasped *by it*. This is transcendent experience.

Just recently I was making a retreat in an area that is a veritable bird sanctuary. I like to pride myself that as a youngster I learned to identify the common species of bird through the kind and patient guidance of a very competent and dedicated lover of nature. But one of the birds on these premises was a stranger to me. My first impulse was to look for a Peterson *Bird Guide* to satisfy my curiosity. Then I realized that none was immediately available and that perhaps the invitation of the moment was to *admire* the reddish markings on the head and tail and to *listen gratefully* to its singular call. I could check out the species at some other time. There would never be another moment like that to admire, wonder, listen and worship.

The lifting of the soul is a nobler way which builds on undersanding, yet transcends it. It responds to the call of beauty, truth, wisdom and love. If we can learn to distinguish one finch from another, can we also wonder at a finch and join the finch in glorifying God? If we can learn how to master the climbing of difficult mountains, can we also sense the beauty of the landscape: the sky and the earth? If the technology of our country can catapult us in a space ship into the outer heavens or onto the moon, do we make the arrogant assertion, "I see no God out here," or do we allow our hearts to be humbled in the realization that "God created the heavens and the earth" (Gn. 1:1)?

A rhythm of life

Initiation into the appreciation of transcendent experience goes beyond merely whetting the appetite for it. It calls for experimenting with a daily and weekly pattern of life which supports this kind of experience. Each of us needs to do what we can to foster an environment which supports a reflective approach to life. This usually means developing a personal rhythm of life which gives inner direction to the various involvements in daily living.

Sometimes we fail to realize how much we surrender the direction of our lives to other people or to the unpredictable development of events. Certainly, there is a real sense in which we eventually want to move beyond the ego-control of life. But in the initial stages of the spiritual journey God asks us to be responsible for introducing certain facilitating conditions for deeper life. For instance, rising early enough to raise the mind and heart to God and to give direction to our day is a significant element in living a transcendent life. Concluding the day with a pause for gratitude, repentance and self-surrender is another ingredient. And frequent participation in the Eucharistic celebration invites us to become more deeply immersed in the most central mysteries of our Christian faith.

So much depends on a personal rule of life if we wish to support a morning lifting of the heart, an evening reflection on the day and regular Eucharistic participation. This personal rule of life will ordinarily involve a concrete commitment to daily extended personal prayer and some supportive reading. What is important is not the bones of our schedule. It is the spirit that we bring to every part of our life: the sense of awe, wonder, growing preference for silence, humor about small things, playfulness and detached industry in approaching our work. These attitudes do not come spontaneously in our culture. They may develop more easily if we can sense these same attitudes in others who model Christian life for us.

As Americans, we tend to become accustomed to a pace of life which is almost violent. It is so demanding that when we stop, we often experience the inner pounding of various untamed impulsive and compulsive drives impelling us into a further round of debilitating activity. Have you ever noticed how the average middle-class American family spends a vacation? Tremendous effort and energy usually go into preparing, packing and mobilizing the family and the appropriate gear. Then there follows the competitive struggle to reach the point of destination in the shortest amount of time and ahead of as many others as possible. There is the task of unpacking and preparing the new locale for the family take-over. By the time people are ready to relax, nerves are frayed and tempers are on edge. Each then scatters in a frantic search for a quick way to calm down and enjoy oneself. The week or two over, everyone enters the same exhausting process in reverse.

Even when we realize what is happening and try to do something about this kind of approach to life, we may find ourselves trapped by the attitudes of others. Everyone also expects a feverish pace of us. People tend to judge our liveliness and attractiveness by our activity. Do we dare to tell a friend that we spent an evening quietly, close to nature, nourished by good reading, providing time for the spirit?

The case of those who enter a novitiate or a seminary is somewhat different. They do not have to take the first initiative in ordering their life anew. They are invited to enter a new routine of life. The regimen usually calls for the basic structures already mentioned. The novitiate normally provides a period of time when serious and sustained academic, pastoral and social involvement is temporarily set aside in order to establish a new rhythm of life. This temporary withdrawal does not imply a denigration of study or pastoral and social involvement. Rather, it provides for a time of relaxed dwelling with transcendent experience, an extended pondering of the common spiritual tradition in the Church and a special immersion in the unique features of the spirituality of one's own institute. Later, the religious may enter into appropriate academic, apostolic and social work in a deeper way. The seminary program, however, usually does not allow for this extended period except through times of common retreat and recollection. The challenge, then, for diocesan seminarians is to utilize these briefer opportunities well and to adopt a daily pattern of life which allows these transcendent values to take on flesh in their daily activities.

The difficulty with the approach of the pre-conciliar past was not in the insistence on some temporary separation from multiple involvements. The problem was the often exaggerated emphasis on *physical* separation and the multiplication of religious activities rather than an emphasis on fostering a transcendent conversion of heart. In our approach today, we need the courage to insist on real solitude and a concrete spiritual regimen, not as ends in themselves, but as graced conditions to facilitate deeper life and greater openness to God, no matter what walk of life God is calling us to pursue.

Love of a personal God

In this movement into transcendent mystery, we are approaching a God who is deeply personal. The Christian experience of transcendence is not vague or abstract or impersonal. It is a meeting with the Triune God.

There may be many obstacles within us that complicate this approach to God. For instance, if we feel guilty, we may experience great anxiety at first about entering into God's presence without defenses. This can be especially true if our previous history has inclined us to perceive God as distant and demanding. Or lingering resentment within us about the way things have developed for us in life can make God seem to be very detached and unconcerned. Anger, then, interposes what seems to be an impassible gulf between us and God.

It is good to ask help in becoming more aware of the obstacles which tend to make God seem remote or less personal. In learning how to express our guilt or resentment or anger to a director, we can learn how to bring these inner experiences to God in prayer. Usually the barriers to intimacy will then begin to crumble. Some will find it helpful to express themselves by writing their prayer to God. What is important is striving to articulate what is really in the heart and truly meaning what is said when approaching God. Simplicity and directness are to be preferred over complicated or elaborate approaches.

God our Father is the personal Creator, Provider and Destiny of our life. He cares profoundly for the least happening in life. He touches the "child" in us and awakens in us the awareness that we depend so completely on parental providence. He evokes trust, surrender, confidence. But it is also true that we may harbor ambivalent attitudes toward human parental love. This seems particularly true for many of us alive today. How helpful it can be to bring these ambivalences, too, to the Father in a direct and humble way. It may even be that some will profit by temporary psychological help in facilitating the healing of more persistent wounds. Ultimately our goal is to make our own the prayer of the psalmist: "Enough for me to keep my soul tranquil and quiet like a child in its mother's arms, as content as a child that has been weaned." (Ps. 131:2)

God the Son, Christ Jesus, is both our Lord and our brother. He has come to become brother to us all. He has experienced human life. He has entered into the mystery of human existence so completely and unequivocally that no dimension of true human experience is foreign to him. We can go to Him as the One who knows and understands our life better than we can ever hope to understand it ourselves. Jesus is more of a brother to us than anyone else can ever be. No matter how many self-doubts may riddle us, no matter how inadequate we may feel, no matter how anxious we may be, Jesus has associated himself with our experience. So we can lay it all at his feet; we can give it over to his healing heart.

Sometimes almost demonic forces seem to keep us from appreciation the redeeming and liberating implications of this Incarnate mystery. Either the freeing impact of this piercing truth is blunted in our life or our attention becomes so riveted on one dimension of Jesus that the other becomes peripheral. Once the divorce of his humanity from his divinity becomes effected, the whole spiritual journey is distorted.

Even as Jesus is our truest brother, he is also our Lord. He is one with each of us; yet he so far transcends mere human nature that we cannot but bow in profound worship. Jesus is Lord of life and death. He is Lord of the heart. Everyone of us has a unique destiny in life that is specifically our own; yet it is caught up also in a destiny that is profoundly the Lord's. He is the Way, the Truth, the Life (Jn.14:6). It is Jesus who brings us to the Father in all our weakness and sinfulness and clothes us in his blood so that we can approach his Father as Jesus himself does.

The road to fuller discipleship of the Lord is challenging. There are so many hurdles and obstacles along the way. John the Apostle offers a succinct picture of the process that the first disciples went through in his kaleidoscopic description of the calling and gradual response of the future apostles (Jn. 1:35-51). First, God used human curiosity and the mediational role of John the Baptist to direct Andrew and John to Jesus. They saw him as an intriguing teacher, a rabbi; in relating all that they had seen and heard to their brothers, Simon and James, they came to call him the Messiah; finally, Nathaniel, after hearing Jesus reveal to him something of his own past, proclaimed Jesus to be the Son of God. In reality, this development took place over a lengthy period of discipleship and only after experiencing Jesus' death, resurrection and the descent of the Spirit. The contemplative John, however, is more interested in inviting the would-be disciple into a preview of the whole journey and then to hearing with the heart the provocative words of Jesus: "What are you looking for?" (Jn. 1:38) and "Come and see" (Jn. 1:39). In one way or another, all of us have to begin by acknowledging what we want most. Then we are invited to come to see Jesus first as a fascinating teacher, then as a unique figure in salvation history and finally as our Lord and God. Prayerful reading, listening to good preaching and the experience of spiritual direction can serve this mysterious call. These aids, like the preaching of John the Baptizer, can point the way. They direct attention to Jesus, his person, his words, his deeds. They encourage us to focus our eyes, ears and heart on the Lord.

In all of this, we are utterly dependent on the light and the empowering grace of God's Holy Spirit. The Spirit is the Paraclete that proceeds both from the Father and the Son and dwells within, enabling a response in faith. The Spirit is divine Gift, unmerited, unearned, undeserved. The Spirit is both deeply within and completely beyond. The Spirit gives life to the whole person. When we speak of spiritual life, we do not mean primarily the life of the *human* spirit. The development of that life can only go so far and always runs the risk of slipping into a false and harmful severance of spirit from body. We really mean human life caught up in God's spiritual life, the life of the Holy Spirit. As Christians, we believe that the gift of the Holy Spirit, offered to all and granted in a unique way in sacrament at baptism, can become an ever more active inner source of redemptive life for the whole person. Thus the Holy Spirit enables us to approach God as *"Abba,* Father'' (Rm. 8:15), leads us to an affirmation in faith that Jesus is Lord (1 Jn. 4:15) and facilitates a way of life marked by the fruits of the Spirit (Gal. 5:22-24).

This is why we ought to be constantly wary of merely external patterns of religious behavior and vigilant for the awakening of true inner life. It is an art to enter into a real discipline of life while keeping our eyes on the greater life which particular disciplines only serve. The role of personal spiritual direction is important, but not central. It aims at helping would-be disciples to be attentive to the more unique ways in which the Holy Spirit directs us. Personal spiritual direction, however, is only one of many ways in which God's Church offers the Spirit's direction in the ministry of word, sacrament and pastoral care. Personal spiritual direction should move toward awakening a unique inner capacity to enter into a life-giving approach to daily life and its rhythms. It also works toward developing the capacity to recognize the deeper truth of the Church's teaching in the Scriptures, in the spiritual tradition, in the mysteries celebrated in sacrament and in the concrete challenges of one's personal vocation. That is why a good spiritual director begs the grace of remaining true to the role of the Baptist. The director calls to a disciplined conversion and then points the way to the Messiah. The director can have a significant role to play; but must not get in the way of the Lord.

The role of meditative prayer

Certainly the intellect is one of the most distinctive and noble gifts of our humanity. To know reality beyond sense experience is unique to the human person among all of tangible creation. But even more wonderful is man's ability to re-know something on a deeper level. This re-knowing emerges from dwelling with a truth, an insight, a thought. Rational knowledge can puff up the human spirit as it increases the inner conviction that reality is coming more and more under our control. But the intellectual knowledge which goes beyond the assimilation of facts and touches the deeper questions has the power to lead to conversion: intellectual, moral and spiritual.

This is especially true of faith-knowledge. The faith facts are few. But it is possible to ponder the truths enshrined in them forever. Meditation is the usual name given to the pondering of faith-truths.

Probably more of us meditate than think we do. Have you ever caught yourself musing about life, its purpose, its destiny, its inconsistencies? It is a normal human experience, although it can be left underdeveloped and undisciplined. When we enter seriously on the spiritual journey, we need to nurture and refine the art of meditation on faith realities.

To begin, it is so important to recognize how much a part of ordinary life meditation already is. The task at hand is not so much to learn something foreign to human experience, but to develop and improve an art that is already incipiently there. The cultivating of an art always involves discipline. And at first a new discipline is awkward or may seem strained. But basically, we want to clarify what makes for *good* musing and can be carried over into meditative prayer.

During the post-Tridentine spiritual renewal, many spiritual masters offered suggested methods toward this purpose. They offered these because people desired a more highly disciplined meditative prayer in the busier life of the newly-emergent city culture. These techniques reflect the greater knowledge of some of the inner processes of mind, imagination and feeling which emerged in the post-Renaissance world. The methods they developed can still be helpful for some.

Perhaps in our own age of complex life, simplicity is the key. Underlying all of the suggestions, there seems to be a common realization that good meditative prayer begins with the experience of inner quieting of the mind and heart, making greater attentiveness to the ever-present God more possible; it continues on to some kind of extended dwelling with an event or a text or a truth; and it moves ultimately toward the awakening of the heart to a desire, determination or affective expression of prayer.

These three movements are basic. In order to approach the Father, we are called to develop the inner single-mindedness and single-heartedness of a child. This involves the stilling of competing desires, thoughts and drives. In order to be united with the Son, we want to become one with the eternal Word spoken. This involves an intelligent musing over the events and words that the Church has handed down in Sacred Scripture and in the spiritual teaching of those recognized as especially reliable interpreters of God's word. In order to receive the gift of the Holy Spirit, we must be willing to make a gift of ourselves in the deeper recesses of our own being. The whole meditative prayer moves toward this culmination in a heart-felt response from the core of our soul. The quieting, as a weaned child before the Father, allows some aspect of the Word to be conceived in the heart and leads to the gifts of the Spirit in a transformed life. Obviously, Mary who not only physically quieted herself before the Father and conceived the Son through the power of the Spirit, but who also spiritually entered a quiet life and then kept the events (Lk. 2:19) and the words (Lk. 2:51) surrounding the mysteries of God in her heart, is the model for Christian meditation.

Some contemporary western Christians, living in a society which keeps a frantic pace of life, have turned in desperation to various approaches, such as the eastern techniques of prayer. Sometimes they miss the more fundamental invitation which is to find the rhythm of life that resists dehumanizing pressures and facilitates greater inner quiet throughout the day. But it may very well be that in this age, the eastern approaches to prayer can be partially helpful in slowing down, experiencing a greater inner calm and making prayer more possible. The erect back, deep rhythmical breathing, the focusing of the eyes and the use of a repetitive phrase do bring inner quietude and attentiveness. If we use any of these approaches, it is important that we not try to come to God artificially. As Christians we want to approach God with all that is going on in our life. We do not want to repress what really needs to be brought to him. These calming techniques can be helpful if they facilitate our going to the Father and placing all cares and anxieties in his hands. Then it may be easier to be receptive to grace and to ponder living truth with less compulsive or impulsive distraction. And it may be easier to respond in self-giving. But the techniques for quieting down are only a propadeutic for prayer. They are not fully Christian prayer in themselves.

Some contemporary western Christians, living in a society that tends to promote alienation rather than communion are also inclined to seek out communal religious experiences which provide the sense of faith-support and love. The faithful living of the Christian life is hard without support. Many Christian adults today feel alone because other adults no longer seem to collaborate in promoting strong faith and moral life. Even as we acknowledge the value of communal support, it is good to recognize that it can be risky to try to avoid the long narrow road to deeper Christian life. Real transformations are nurtured and strengthened in the quiet of the heart and the courageous struggle with the challenges of everyday living. Quick conversions and artificial community can provide an uplifting experience for a time. The real transformation involves the intelligent activation of the center of a human being—what the Scriptures call the heart—and moves toward humble and contrite yielding to God.

There are two extremes to avoid: if we bypass the intellect, we risk the development of an empty-headed spirituality; if we remain in the intellect alone without moving on to the heart, we risk the development of a highly-intellectualized spirituality. Meditative prayer, properly understood and practiced, is the narrow passageway that helps us navigate between Scylla and Charybdis.

Finally, it may be appropriate to note at this time that meditative prayer should eventually become even more simplified if we are faithful to the experience. As we become more accustomed to quieting down before our God, we will extend the spirit of recollection more and more to the rest of our activity. Then, when we return to the moments of more explicit prayer, we will not have to delay with this first movement. Moreover, as the spirit of recollection pervades more and more of our life, we will find ourselves enlightened and drawn into prayer by fewer words. Thus we will move more quickly through both the quieting of the soul and the listening with the heart toward the affective response. This development is toward a prayer of presence, a prayer of simplicity, sometimes called acquired contemplation.

The first movement in the spiritual life, then, is growing in a greater communion with God. God is so loving and inviting. Yet we tend to allow so many obstacles to get in the way. The asceticism of moving gently, yet firmly into transcendent awareness helps to minimize the difficulties which arise both from within and without. The meditative experience helps us to become more enlightened about the real God and eventually leads us to more simplified prayer.

One of the most common stumbling blocks to deeper life is failing to take these steps very seriously. We can presume that we already know God. Or we can shy away from the effort involved in cooperating with God's invitations to a more disciplined approach to Him.

Only if we truly begin to meet God as He truly is, will the spiritual journey become more attractive. Only if we meet God within, will our spiritual discipline become life-giving. Living a spiritual regimen with a distorted understanding of God or without inner religious experience leads to superficial and often neurotic religious practice. This eventually makes the true life of the Spirit less accessible.

Once we have been truly moved within by the Real God, the inner life is enkindled . . . and we are drawn to seek deeper conversion of heart.

DEEPENING CONVERSION OF HEART

Probably the greatest enemy to authentic faith life is not atheism, but *distorted* religious practice. No human device could be a more effective decoy in diverting people from life-giving religious truth. This seems to be especially true when it comes to the call to conversion. There is nothing that human nature craves more than the transformation which the experience of God's personal, healing love can bring. Yet so few seem to be able to help others truly to find this grace. Ambivalence over what is really sin, a burdensome anxiety over free-floating guilt, confusion over the proper approach to the sacraments of healing, a tendency to reduce sin to manageable proportions by rigid formulae or to deny most sin altogether in the name of human self-development, all these and more have robbed us of the grace we crave most: to hear the good news that our sins are truly forgiven.

An insight into the plight of a contemporary man is offered by Albert Camus in his novel, *The Fall.* Jean-Baptiste Clemence had been living two lives, one public as a competent lawyer and generous humanitarian, the other private and full of moral compromise. Somehow he had been able to muffle the faint cries of his repressed spirit begging for liberation and reconciliation. He had come to live with this unfortunate truce with relative ease. But one night when crossing a bridge, he witnessed a young woman plunge from the lofty structure and slip into the icy Seine. He cast a quick glance around and saw no one looking. He suppressed the call to heroic courage and personal risk and hurried on. But the experience of that night haunted him ever after. The professional lawyer became a "judge-penitent," that is, he found himself compelled to spend his nights in taverns, drowning his guilt in alcohol and compulsively confessing the duplicity of his life to any willing ear while judging harshly the lives of others. There seemed to be no escape from the awful burden of his guilt.

Do we experience something of this burden of sin? Do we sense a vague heaviness about guilt? Do we find ourselves confused, anxious, uncertain about how to handle the guilt? Are we inclined to plunge into a perpetual round of activities rather than risk the uneasiness which tends to surface when we try to slow down and face ourselves?

No matter who we are, we experience some difficulty with sin. But, if we desire to enter into deeper life, we want to allow ourselves to approach this area of life in simplicity and transparency of heart. It is less and less possible for us to grow up innocent of the evil that tends to engulf us, even though we may be quite naive about the reality of sin. If we are truly meeting God in prayer without defenses or pretensions, we will begin to be aware of how God sees us, loves us and wants us more free from the power of sin.

The glory to which we are called

The way in which people view human nature usually has a profound impact on the approach they take to sin. Thus Camus' existential pessimism is reflected in the story he tells of Jean-Baptiste Clemence, who, although he carried both the Baptist's name and the word for mercy in his own name, could not find anyone to point the way to repentance and mercy.

That is why from early times, Christians have been trying to understand how God views human nature. Hence they have asked themselves what it means to hear or read the Scriptural word: "God created man in the image of himself, in the image of God he created him, male and female he created them" (Gn. 1:27).

Their meditative pondering of this faith-fact led some of the early Christian thinkers to recognize that there was an image theme recurrent throughout the Scriptures. God has created us in his own image (Gn. 1:27). Unfortunately the image was gravely tarnished through sin (Gn. 3). In this fallen state the prophets warned consistently against substituting any other image in the form of an idol (Is. 2:20; 31:7; 48:5. Jer. 50:38). Eventually Paul was to assert that Jesus Christ is the perfect "image of the unseen God and the first born of all creation" (Col. 1:15) and that all things are to be reconciled through him and for him (Col.1:20).

Subsequently, a whole series of great Christian thinkers took up the theme and explored further what it might mean. In summary they concluded that there is a very real imprint of the Trinitarian God in us. First, at the core of the human person is a heart, the deepest part of the person, the origin of direction, purpose and unity; this is an image of the Father. Secondly, we have a mind capable of laying-hold of life-giving truth; this is an image of the Son. Thirdly, we have the capacity to make a gift of ourselves in love; this is an image of the Holy Spirit. This triune divine image reveals the great glory of the human person, a glory that endows us with a unique dignity and foreshadows the grandeur of our destiny in life. This is how God created and wanted us to be.

This divine image lost its likeness with the primeval sin (Gn. 3). Thereafter, we lost the experience of wholeness and instead began to know a very painful inner dividedness. The intended experience of unity and harmony in the depths of the human person gave way to inner conflicts and painful disharmony. The intended movement of the mind toward the truth that sets us free became confused by half-truths and frustrated by ignorance. The intended free movement of the will toward

CENTER

altruistic self-giving became locked in patterns of self-protective rigidity or apathetic narcissism.

In this wounded state, people were morally crippled until the saving appearance of Jesus Christ. In Christ the distorted image was destroyed. For his heart was focused in a singular way on his Father's purpose; his mind grasped life-giving truth which he shared with others; his will enabled him to make a complete gift of himself both to his Father and to all people.

All of us, the Apostle tells us, are invited to participate in this restoration of the image of God in us. We are incorporated into the restored image in Baptism (Rm. 8:28). But the *experience* of restoration comes only slowly and gradually as we enter seriously and perseveringly on the spiritual journey of conversion.

The experience of sin

The foregoing offers us a rich understanding of our true nobility and the most important call we have received. It is the prayerful reading of the classical spiritual writings that inspires us with this vision. It is prayer that leads us to sense both the attractiveness of the teaching and the distance we experience between the dream and our present plight. The contemplation of the glory of our origin and destiny as well as the nobility of our own unique selves actually make it more attractive to bring to God whatever may be distorting his image in us or arousing our anxiety in his presence.

Entrance into conversion of heart can never be forced. It is important that we *want* to become more immersed in the Christ-life. It is necessary to be faithful in approaching God in prayer. We need to beg for fuller redemption. But it is a grace, a gift of God. We cannot demand it. We cannot accomplish conversion on our own. All we can do is to persevere in coming to him as authentically and unpretentiously as we can.

In the continuing efforts to meet the Lord Jesus in prayer, we will gradually become more aware with St. Paul that "instead of doing the good things I want to do, I carry out the sinful things I do not want" (Rm. 7:19). This consciousness of inner dividedness usually follows close upon the awakened desire to follow Christ more unreservedly.

The divided self begins to manifest itself in many disappointing ways. We become more and more aware how little harmony really exists in us. We start to recognize how little we truly know ourselves. It becomes clearer how easy we can deceive ourselves. Motivation seems so complex. Life-giving truth seems so elusive.

In a special way our moral disorientation seems to be rooted in ego-centrism. The *original* sin has become a diabolical paradigm for all other sin. Ego-centrism closes off the call to transcendent existence. As a result, we sense that the call of the Spirit to unfamiliar, higher life is

A Practical Guide To Spiritual Formation

too risky. It seems safer to remain on the more familiar terrain. So, as fallen human beings, we set ourselves up as our own gods, the ultimate arbiters of moral good, the principal beneficiaries of our own efforts and designs. We are inclined to set out on the road of strengthening and fortifying our own egos to handle the stress and strain of life more successfully. We may seek to develop ourselves in as many ways as possible to extend our mastery over life—our own and that of others.

Contemporary western culture which exalts self-development as an ideal can feed into this fundamental disorientation unless a key distinction is recognized. There is a wholesome maturation of the individual which eventually reaches its culmination in self-giving and self-transcendence. On the other hand there is a narcissistic cult of personal gifts that leads to extreme individualism and self-centeredness. What is the difference? The parable of the talents offers us a clue (Mt. 25:14-30). In this parable Jesus made it clear that the talents were gifts given in trust; they were not personal possessions. The trading with the talents which Jesus lauded was not a self-serving amassing of personal riches or successes, but an enterprising approach which grew out of a realization that what had been received was a gift to be used constructively and ultimately to be accounted for at the appropriate time. Life, too, is a gift, received in trust, to be responded to creatively, but ultimately to be given back with its fruit. There is a tremendous difference between individualistic attempts at self-aggrandizement and the humble, forthright use of giftedness in a responsible way to help others.

As we become more aware of our ego-centrism, we slowly begin to sense, in contrast to the ideals of the gospel call, that there are real areas of sinfulness in ourselves. We recognize our own moral weakness and our great need for healing from above. The dividedness extends to many of our approaches to life: our envy, our greed, our hostility, our intemperance, our lust, our apathy. Thus envy becomes manifest in our radical difficulty in truly believing that God loves us uniquely and personally; hence our self-doubt moves us to covet what others seem to be or have. Greed takes over when our trust in God is so fragile that we need to surround ourselves with all of the supports which the world offers us in order to ensure security for the uncertain future. Anger, instead of being directed constructively against the powers of evil and in service to good, may be diverted in a destructive way towards ourselves or others. Intemperance and lust tend to sabotage the kind of friendly communion of body and spirit which makes it possible for the body to support deeper inner life and for the spirit to be sacramentalized in the way we use our bodies. Apathy bespeaks, not the peace of rich life in the Lord, but the inertia of a deadened spirit.

All these fundamental disorientations are present at least latently within us. They tend to infect our personal relationships with others. They even have an impact on our relationships to the economic, political, and social structures of society. For, as suggested in Camus' *The Fall,* the unhealed dividedness of pesonal life can subvert commitment to public acts of integrity.

Self-knowledge in these areas comes very slowly. It is the fruit, less of harsh self-scrutiny, and more of a humble dialogue between the real self and the transcendent God. It is gentle and freeing even though greater depths of sinfulness may be uncovered and the need for greater healing experienced. If we tend to be hard on ourselves, scrupulous or introspective, we may need to be helped to move beyond this to a more reverent and accepting attitude.

Obstacles to deeper conversion

Harshness toward ourselves can sometimes seriously hamper true conversion. Usually it is due to a lack of self-acceptance. Emerging self-knowledge does not automatically move to wholesome self-acceptance. Part of the difficulty may rest in an inability to appreciate fully the implications of the divided self inherited from birth and further wounded in life-experience. We find ourselves truly divided between the call to be true to the real self and the temptation to yield to the false, disoriented self. The real self bears the imprint of God's image. It is deeply loved by God. The false self bears the image of sin, original and personal. God wants to diminish the power of the false self. We have a poor self-image if we only focus on the image of sin and, on the one hand, either see ourselves harshly as all bad or, on the other, over-compensate for the evil by exhibiting an artificial bravado about our supposed goodness. A healthy self-image accepts the co-presence of good and evil, sees the good as more true and more real and knows that God so deeply loves the true self that he wishes to purify and heal the false self of its sinful distortions. We enter more gently into this genuine self-acceptance, if we remind ourselves that God's healing is always partial in this life; complete only in the life to come.

Another obstacle to deeper conversion arises from a human tendency to remain in a very immature stage of moral conscience development. As children we had to learn right and wrong from parental figures who reinforced right choices with acceptance and discouraged wrong choices with disapproval. There is no other way we could have been introduced to incipient moral life. The difficulty comes when we fail to move beyond the moral consciousness of a child and become arrested in our development on a childish level. Thus we can find ourselves principally preoccupied with fostering moral behavior which meets the approval of significant adult figures and fulfills the obvious prescriptions of the law. This approach to moral life constricts the life of the inner spirit and keeps us basically on the outside of religious practice. Incidentally, this approach to moral life not only severely limits the individuals involved, but also makes religious practice unattractive to others. Hence it is so important for us who intend to move into public ministry in the Church to seek out help in moving beyond this immaturity.

The invitation of God to mature in the moral life can lead us into another trap. The need to be free of childish moralizing prompts us to become more interior. As we try to interiorize moral decision-making, we can begin to slip into that experience of ego-centrism which makes our own egos the center of moral life. We can begin to decide that what seems to promote self-development is always good and what seems to stand in the way of self-development is evil. Moral decision-making, thus, becomes interior, but unfortunately, self-referring. We may not be so clearly aware that what we are taking pains to develop is our *divided* self. Some of the more humiliating developments in my life have occurred when I came to realize that what I was developing so painstakingly in myself supposedly for the service of others contained also much potential for evil. And the potential for evil was in a sense more powerful because it was more hidden. For instance, celibate life, so wholesome in itself, can cloak a tendency to keep people at an emotional distance and even to use people for personal advantage. Or probably the greatest danger at this level is hardness of heart. We do not sense so poignantly our own need to be redeemed and so we are inclined to keep God at a distance. Being a courteous God, he respects our freedom profoundly and will not force himself on us.

Can we move beyond childish and adolescent levels of moral life to an adult approach? Can we sense that behind the often imperfectly expressed moral norms the Church offers us, there are life-giving truths to live? Can we accept the challenge to subjective interiorization in order to move beyond merely external religion? The history of salvation, old and new, records for us a pattern: God reveals his moral truth; after a while people begin to package it neatly in concise, clear-cut norms, encouraging a childish morality; then some people revolt and throw off the rigid patterns of living as untrue to inner freedom; finally, inspired figures re-express the original revelation in a deeper, life-giving way. As we recognize the direction in which God calls us, we will participate more and more in the adult approach to moral truth and life.

The sacrament of reconciliation

It is possible that sometimes we may rush too quickly to the sacrament of reconciliation. We may need to dwell more with the conversion movement. The only authentic way we can approach God is as loved sinners. This may mean that we need to stay with the experience of being loved—or we may need to allow ourselves to sense more interiorly the depths of our need. But it is in a prayerful, loving approach to our saving God that the best contrition is nourished. We want to give ourselves over to him humbly, gently and trustingly.

We know that God offers us a sacrament of his continuing desire to purify, forgive and heal in this sacrament of reconciliation. In baptism, the fundamental grace of conversion has been granted. But in this sacrament of healing there is an on-going expression of God's caring love and reassuring fidelity. God wants to help us to continue that humble communion with transcendent Love.

The Church's pastoral decision to offer this sacrament more frequently seems to have emerged from the wisdom of the early ascetics who discovered that a humble acknowledging of the inner evil desires, thoughts and inclinations strengthened the inner self and disarmed the enemy. The sacramental context made God's redemptive love more tangible and increased the awareness of the ecclesial and social dimensions to both sin and grace.

Probably no other sacramental encounter gives a more accurate picture of where we may be on the journey to God. The minister of this sacrament has a most sacred trust. The seal of confession obviously requires the priest to keep what is revealed in utter confidence. Above and beyond the explicit sins confided, we share implicitly with the confessor the nature of our approach to God; how we experience God; how free we are to acknowledge sin; how well we know ourselves; how much we sense God's love for us. In effect, something of our whole inner relationship to God, to ourselves and to others becomes manifest. The reverent confessor accepts this in humility and treats it as sacred; he responds in a way that facilitates the grace of healing appropriate to our need.

Obviously, sin can be forgiven in many different ways: personal repentance, reparaton for harm done others, personal prayer, mortification, the forgiveness of others, deeds of charity, a contrite celebration of the Eucharist. But in this sacrament of reconciliation there is a special grace that flows from our greater consciousness of God's love, our explicit acknowledgement of our own personal sinfulness, our facing of the ramifications of both sin and grace in our lives with others and our recognition of the truth that grace in the new covenant is especially ecclesial.

A director has a special opportunity to facilitate a periodic approach to this sacrament as a graced way to assist the experience of personal conversion. Inevitably there will be some obstacles which make this difficult for different individuals. Sometimes bad confessional experiences in the past have left deep wounds. Sometimes rigid confessional practices have robbed the penitent of a deeper sense of the power and freedom of a more wholesome approach. Sometimes a lack of much experience of confession in the past simply makes it frightening and mysterious. Many today are dissatisfied with the routine approach they have previously followed, but have not yet found a satisfactory substitute. Whatever the experience may have been in the past, we are dealing here with fostering a more wholesome relationship between continuing conversion and sacramental reality. The most important invitation that the renewed rite of this sacrament calls us to, is the spirit of faith, humility and worship which ought to mark both the attitude of confessor and penitent in celebrating this sacrament.

The fruits of true conversion

There is an incident in the gospel account of Jesus' ministry which reverses the Camus tale. It is the conversion of Zaccheus (Lk. 19:1-10). Apparently Zaccheus, too, had been living a double life, on the one hand as a successful public figure and yet on the other as a man involved in fraud and extortion. The eyes of Jesus met his as he climbed a sycamore tree to get a good view of this remarkable man. That glance touched something very deep within and called forth a desire for a new life. Jesus recognized that power had touched Zaccheus and asked him simply for the privilege of dining with him. Zaccheus opened his heart and home, publicly pledged reparation in the presence of his friends and embarked on a new life of grace. The experience of Jesus' loving glance had led to a conversion of heart; conversion led to a single-heartedness, wisdom and the desire for total dedication.

The fruit of authentic conversion is inner joy and freedom for a more whole-hearted response. There is no happiness to compare with it. For the heaviest burden we carry is our own sin and the sin of others. Jesus makes it utterly clear that the first fruit of the resurrection is the gift of the Spirit that brings peace and forgiveness of sin (Jn. 20:22-23).

We can identify other fruits of true conversion in another incident recorded in John's gospel. Many scholars consider it to be an interpolation, coming possibly from the Lucan corpus instead of the fourth gospel. In any case the Church has affirmed it to be authentically integral to the inspired account of Jesus' life and ministry. It is the description of the meeting between Jesus and the woman caught in adultery (Jn. 8:1-11). It is obvious from the introductory remarks to this episode that the scribes and Pharisees wanted to trap Jesus. He had preached mercy toward the sinner; yet the Law was utterly clear in cases where the adultery of a woman could be publicly attested. Jesus refused to be pinned on the horns of the dilemma. In effect he asked the accusers to look into themselves; namely, "If there is one of you who has not sinned, let him be the first to cast a stone at her" (Jn. 8:7). And they slipped away one by one. Then that remarkable and touching exchange transpired: "Jesus looked up and said, 'Woman, where are they? Has no one condemned you?' 'No one, sir,' she replied. 'Neither do I condemn you,' said Jesus, 'go away and do not sin any more.' "

Two comments seem especially appropriate here: Jesus revealed how

God shows mercy without condoning sin; Jesus uncovered the sad plight of those who, seeing no need for repentance in themselves, are inclined to show no mercy to others. This is an episode worth pondering.

True conversion, although profoundly personal and interior, has a way of manifesting itself. It will be revealed in our attitude toward sin in others. Camus' Jean-Baptiste Clemence could not experience divine forgiveness; so, he became a "judge-penitent." He poured out his confession to others in the form of a harsh judgment on the world. The sermon on the mount, at first reading, seems to suggest that the disciple is enjoined not to judge so that he can avoid judgement (Mt. 7:1). The fuller truth, however, is that the inner reluctance to judge or condemn another is the *fruit* of the transforming experience of being freely forgiven for sin that called for real condemnation. Jesus did not ask us to develop will-power in order to control our tendency to condemn others in moral judgement. The parable of the unforgiving debtor makes this clear (Mt. 18:23-35). Rather, Jesus invites us to the banquet of mercy that we might be *freed* to bestow mercy on our brothers and sisters. Forgiving those who trespass against us is the fruit of being forgiven our own trespasses (Mt. 6:12). True conversion, then, leads to great compassion.

Conversion of the heart has the power to transform human relationships. It leads to humility before God because the heart recognizes that only God can save; it leads to patience with ourselves because the heart now knows it cannot save itself; it leads to compassion for the weakness and sinfulness of others because the heart senses instinctively that it has been forgiven so much. That is why, too, true Christian conversion leads to the expanding life of charity.

EXPANDING THE LIFE OF CHARITY

Growing communion with God and deepening conversion of heart are the basis for true Christian charity. St. Augustine has particularly helped to make this clear for us. He was so painfully aware of the wrong way of loving in his early life, that he made a special point of sharing his own experience to illustrate what he meant. Despite the popular misunderstanding in this regard, Augustine did not equate the wrong way of loving with sexually promiscuous behavior. Rather he distinguished between *eros* and *agape*. For him, eros was self-regarding, self-referring love, an expression of narcissism. *Agape* was self-transcending, self-giving love, an expression of a truly altruistic reaching-out for God and others.

The experiences which led him to his conclusions are recorded for us in his *Confessions*. The book is a remarkable document. Written in his mid-forties by a man who had just been appointed bishop of Hippo, this book represents his determined desire to walk *with* his people as a fellow Christian, even as he was designated bishop *for* them. Lest he ever become proud or forget his past, he laid his soul bare for the people. The whole treatise is a prayer of confession: in praise of God for his wondrously faithful and merciful love for him and in repentance of the labyrinthine ways in which he had run in frantic search for self-gratification. In the central eighth book, Augustine offers a dramatic account of the triumph of God's relentless pursuit of him. The journey of years came to a climax. All the obstacles seemed to disintegrate: the issue of freedom; the problem of evil; the struggle with the flesh; the difficulty with the Scriptures and Church teaching. Augustine was moved in the very depths of his heart and collapsed in grateful tears of liberation. He had come to realize that real love was not his love of the flesh, nor his love for worldly success, nor even his love for learning. He experienced real love only when he accepted God's personal, faithful love for him.

What he learned in the crucible of life, Augustine reflected on at great length. Eventually he wrote the *City of God* to express his understanding of the journey of all society to God. It is here that he contrasted the city of God and the city of man. This was not basically a pitting of the Church against the world. Rather, it was a dissertation on the differences between two kinds of loving: *agape* and cupidity. He recognized that every man is capable of both. In fact, they co-exist in the same person although one always becomes more dominant. The call of the Christian is to move beyond the control of self-serving love or cupidity toward the God-inspired love of *agape.* What the ordinary individual experiences in this struggle in a personal way becomes acted out in society on a much more global level. The struggles among nations are a macrocosm of the struggles of individuals. Augustine's experience taught him that the graced breakthrough of a transcendent God into life is the key to conversion of heart and that conversion of heart opened up the real possibility for Christian charity.

Trinitarian love

The same Augustine who left us this testimony of his own discoveries about the origin and grounding of charity, recommended that we contemplate Trinitarian love to grow in our appreciation of true charity. He was convinced that it is fundamentally the grace of our Triune God that makes it possible for us to come together in self-giving rather than self-serving relationships. His testimony can be a helpful reminder to us to begin in the right place. *Agape* is of transcendent origin.

Who can speak or write about God's love? It is unfathomable. Whatever is said falls so far short of the reality that it almost becomes more untrue than true. This is the reason for the apophatic tradition in spirituality. Eventually we must proceed beyond all conceptual and rational knowledge to reach God. The great mystics have been accustomed to resort to sense language to express this supra-conceptual and supra-rational experience. They speak of hearing, seeing, tasting, touching, even smelling God.

If it were not for the revelation in Jesus Christ, we would have no inkling whatsoever of the Trinitarian nature of god. Once it had been revealed, it was possible for the inspired writers to recognize the Trinitarian image in human nature. But we never could have realized this on our own. Even with this revelation, extremely little is known of the inner life of God. For revelation concerns itself primarily with God's self-communication to the world.

Enlightened initially by Christ and the Scriptures, aided by the reflections of deep Christian thinkers and guided by the wisdom of the Church, it is possible to have some slight glimpse into Trinitarian love: the Father knew himself so perfectly and conceived from all eternity his Son, and the eternal mutual love which binds the Father and Son is the Holy Spirit. There is a community of persons and unity in being. The love is eternal, mutual, distinctive, reverential. It so transcends human experience that the human heart can only pause and wonder in silent adoration.

Incarnational love

But Trinitarian love did not remain solely an intra-Trinitarian mystery. Divine love became creative. What the Father created became reality through the Son in the power of the Spirit. This was true of the universe as a whole, of the human race in particular and in a unique way of the humanity of Jesus Christ. The Father overshadowed the Virgin Mary; she conceived of the Holy Spirit and bore the Son of God (Lk. 2:32, 35). It is a truth that defies simplistic explanations. It is a fact that evokes awe, wonder and worship. Matthew and Luke captured the human picture; John and Paul focused on the transcendent reality. And Christians over the centuries have bowed to ponder, lifted their hearts in joy, tried to express the mystery in painting or sculpture or music or poetry.

The inspired author of the letter to the Hebrews offered an insight into the inner mind which had prompted this extraordinary marriage between God and man when he suggested that the words of the psalmist were in Christ's heart as he entered this life: "You who wanted no sacrifice or oblation prepared a body for me. You took no pleasure in holocausts or sacrifices for sin; then I said, just as I was commanded in the scroll of the book, 'God, here I am! I am coming to obey your will' " (Hb. 10:5-7). And Paul taught that although "his state was divine, yet he did not cling to his equality with God but emptied himself to assume the condition of a slave, and became as men are; and being as men are, he was humbler yet, even to accepting death, death on a cross . . ." (Phil. 2:6-8).

The incarnational love of God was very concrete. Each event, each word, each action expressed inner consecrated love. The events moved inexorably to the climax which is recalled and recelebrated each year during Holy Week and Easter. The Church continually presents these mysteries to the faithful to contemplate and live. Christ's love was not saccharine. His was a strong, sacrificial love that did not hesitate to offer all in fulfillment of the redemptive plan of love.

Liturgical mystery

How are we to enter into the mystery of this Divine Love? The apostles faced this same question in the first generation Church. Their understanding of their mandate was to preach the divine condescension in Jesus Christ and to celebrate this mystery in sacrament. Our attentive listening to good preaching strengthens our belief in the great mysteries. Liturgical life mediates between transcendent mystery and human experience. Symbol is expressive of a reality that no literal human word can fully grasp. It partly expresses but partly only suggests the truth which it signifies. Unlike ordinary symbols, a sacrament actually makes the mystery *present* and available in a special way for us.

We, then, need to appreciate how baptism truly unites us to Christ's incarnational life and paschal love. It is more than ritual. It is initiation into his life. What in baptism has happened in sacrament can be more fully appropriated and experienced as the disciple truly enters more and more into the Christ-life.

Like baptism, confirmation strengthens us in the gift of the Spirit and the living of the life of God. It confirms us in his call to discipleship and a particular life call that is peculiar to us. A clearer discernment of this unique call comes gradually as we try more and more to respond to the life of the Spirit and to interpret the concrete ways in which God reveals his face to us.

Spiritual immersion in sacramental reality is so very central. It presupposes an incipient openness to the transcendent. We want to approach liturgical and sacramental prayer with awe and humility. These are moments of being taught by God through the Church and being drawn into transcendent mystery. So much depends on our approach to liturgical life. Liturgical prayer is first of all a *given,* not a public prayer to be created *ex nihilo* by the participants. It is a time to let go of an excessive ego-management of life and be taught and moved by the Holy Spirit. Liturgical prayer is ecclesial prayer; that is, it is the communion of Christ's disciples praying with him to the Father in the Spirit. It is a school of prayer in that the heart which is open to being taught is going to be enlightened more and more about how to be united with Christ, how to worship the Father in life and how to be led by the Spirit.

It is laudable to recognize that we who enter into Church ministry have a special call to offer the Church's morning and evening prayer. This is especially true for deacons, priests and religious who assume a public responsibility in this regard. But it is even more to the point to emphasize the critical importance of the *way* we pray. If we are praying with others, let the pace make personal involvement in the prayer more possible. If we are praying alone, we need to resist the temptation to rush through mere words and allow ourselves the opportunity to dwell with the prayer even if that means we do not complete the entire text at a given time. Whether alone or with others, we want to remember that this is ecclesial prayer offered in and with and for the whole Church.

Eucharistic prayer is the source and summit of Christian life. What it is in theory becomes reality to the extent that we really enter into the mystery of God's great self-giving in Christ Jesus. It is unwise to focus a great deal of attention on the externals of celebration except to ensure that they are reverent, reasonably ordered and supportive of prayerful involvement in the mystery that is offered. The Eucharist is a gift that is to be received with awe and gratitude. Hence it is very important to direct attention, not to self-expression, but to God's self-giving. A great deal of energy channelled into creative expressions in Eucharistic celebration may be seriously misplaced. The energy and effort are better directed to fostering simple and contemplative supports for personal involvement in Eucharistic prayer. Each day we come to the Eucharist in further need of redemptive healing; each day we are offered some spiritual teaching about the mysteries God has revealed; each day the Lord Jesus, by the power of the Spirit, offers himself anew in sacramental sacrifice to the Father for our sake; each day we beg through the priest for the gift of the Spirit to transform our lives and enable us to worship in truth in our daily living with others; each day a climax comes in the Lord's sacramental gift of himself in a communion, profoundly intimate, healing and restorative. A prayerful approach to the celebration of the Eucharist can strengthen our appreciation of these inexhaustible riches.

Liturgical life and sacramental mystery, therefore, call us to recognize that all of life is sacramental. We are called to live a human life which is open to the divine from birth to death. All life is sacred, the gift of divine Love. All human life is to be lived as an expression of divine love.

The love of one another

No one could possibly make the invitation to love clearer or express it with more force than John the Apostle: "Let us love one another, since love comes from God and everyone who loves is begotten by God and knows God" (1 Jn.4:7). We are exhorted to fraternal charity, a charity that originates, not with ourselves, but with God. Just as the love of God is "not our love for God, but God's love for us when he sent his son to the sacrifice that takes our sins away" (1 Jn. 4:10), so the motive for love of one another is that "God has loved us so much" (1 Jn. 4:11). "We are to love, then, because he loved us first. Anyone who says, 'I love God,' and hates his brother is a liar since a man who does not love the brother that he can see cannot love God, whom he has never seen" (1 Jn. 4:19-20).

It was Jesus himself who revealed that intimate relationship between accepting God's love and our loving one another. In a special way he made it utterly clear in the washing of the feet at the Last Supper. In effect, he asked each apostle to accept personally the gift of his saving love as he washed his feet individually. It was a symbolic washing, expressing Jesus' desire to love and save each disciple as John makes clear in his report of the moving dialogue between Jesus and Simon Peter (Jn. 13:6-11). Then, after Jesus had completed acting out what really was a parable in action, he asked them: "Do you understand what I have done to you? You call me Master and Lord, and rightly; so I am. If I then, the Lord and Master, have washed your feet, you should wash each other's feet. . . . I give you a new commandment: love one another; just as I have loved you, you also must love one another'' (Jn. 13:12-14; 34). The Old Covenant had called for whole-hearted love of God (Dt. 6:5) and love for the neighbor as oneself (Lv. 19:18). But Jesus asked us to love one another as *he* has loved us.

Unfortunately, sometimes in catechetical instruction, the teaching on the Christian moral life is separated from the teaching on the life of faith, hope and charity. In fact, it is often treated apart from sacramental and mystical life, too. But the exigency to love others does not flow from some isolated moral imperative uttered by Christ. Rather, Christ pointed to the inner transformation which the experience of God's total self-giving can release in us. That is why contemplation of God's love can never be severed from true Christian action without doing violence to the uniqueness of Christian life. It is the graced conversion of heart that makes true Christian charity more possible.

It is in this context that Augustine's distinction between a love of *eros* and a love of *agape* looms large. The love of others that is not grounded in God's love tends to be manipulative, seductive or self-serving in some way. Only the love that is grounded in God begins to move beyond selfishness to more genuine care for others in God.

Efforts directed primarily at facilitating or improving our life with others can be self-defeating if they do not recognize that common life is a share in the Trinitarian common life, that the origin, source and sustainer of this life is God and that the principal obstacles to deeper shared life have more to do with the need for personal conversion leading to more communion rather than merely external human communication. Once the authentic ground is established, then skills and techniques can provide a helpful refinement of human interaction.

Expansive Christian love

Although Christian charity meets its most important test with the people with whom we live, charity is not restrictive in scope. Like God's own expansive love which did not remain exclusively an intra-Trinitarian love, charity reaches out in expanding circles of caring concern. The Christian disciple is called to care for friends, for co-workers, for those in need, for people throughout the world. There seem to be concentric circles of concern which become larger and larger as the heart expands in true charity.

The enlarging of the horizons of concern cannot be at the expense of the more primary charity toward those at home. The different levels of commitment into which we enter can help to clarify priorities in practice. For all Christians, the love of God comes first. Married men and women are called to keep their consecration to spouse and family in the next place; religious owe their next priority to their community; the priest to his people and the priestly fraternity. Then the claims of parents, relatives, co-workers and associates fall into place. We Christians cannot let our horizons become too limited. Everyone in need is neighbor to us, as Jesus indicated in the parable of the good Samaritan (Lk. 10:29-37).

It is possible that at times the call of conscience may make the observance of these priorities in love more difficult. Jesus did not promise to eliminate such tensions (Mt. 10:34-36). But the presence of tension does not render these priorities less binding. The true prophet loves his native community and remains within it even under stress and in the face of rejection.

Another challenge to these priorities can come from friendship. Normally, friendships emerge from within these various circles of concerned love. Friendship is truly a gift. It can spring up between people spontaneously no matter how close or distant the external relationship may have been. It usually invites affective development and brings a strengthening of personality. To the extent that friendship truly involves a mutual reverence, respect and support for the loves that are primary in life, it can truly nurture and strengthen deeper life. Only if friendship begins to move two people into such exclusivity and mutual preoccupation that more fundamental commitments are in jeopardy, does friendship become harmful.

In our present age, hopefully, we have a clearer sense that the claim of those in need refers not only to individuals, but to whole classes or races or groupings of people. Concern for justice is constitutive of the church's mission and the preaching of the gospel. We need to expand our vision and our love to encompass all. In practice, we will have to distinguish between opening the heart to all in need and giving ourselves to those particular services which may be appropriate to our personal vocation and gifts. If we are in training, we are going to be called to recognize that the quality and fruitfulness of our charity will depend on temporarily restricting our focus during the graced period when our attention is directed to deeper communion with God and a more profound conversion of life. If love does not become expansive, it is not fully Christian; if it draws us too far away from the divine Source of charity or those who have primary claim on our love, it runs the risk of becoming less and less explicitly Christian.

The urgent demands in society today for more adequate safeguards for peace, more just economic, political and social structures, a more equitable distribution of the world's goods and more reverence for human life, cry out for serious Christian attention. If we can open wide our hearts to God and our fellow man in holy concern and if we can make our limited contributions, consonant with our own vocational callings, it will encourage those whose primary gift it is to lead in these areas to build a kingdom of greater peace and justice on earth.

In preparing for Church ministry, we have a real challenge in this area. Our instinct, at first, may be to multiply social involvements. This has the advantage of expanding horizons and avoiding a narrow and myopic preoccupation. However, extensive involvement brings its own handicaps. It tends to capture our primary attention and makes it more difficult to experience the silence which is a condition for deeper prayer and the desert which is the context for greater self-knowledge and a more pervasive conversion in life. The goal is to expand the heart while disciplining the helping hand. Anthony of the desert instructs his would-be ascetics why it is that so many who begin the spiritual journey with great enthusiasm, lose their way and end in confusion or disaster. Too few have the humility to learn from the experience of those who have gone before them. Then, lacking discretion and balance, they either proceed with brash self-confidence or else never embrace the necessary discipline to help them move beyond the start.[1]

The uneven road to Christian charity

We, too, might ask: how can we learn from those who have gone before us as we try to face the contemporary challenges of growing in Christian love? We know that the apostle Paul, in writing his first letter to the troubled Christian community, made clear what are the characteristics of genuine charity: patience, kindness, humility, reverence, altruism, joy in the truth, forgiveness, trust, hope and endurance (cf. 1 Cor. 13: 4-7). We know, too, that Augustine offered to the world a vivid contrast between cupidinous love and *agape*. What are the difficulties we are apt to meet as we seek to grow in this charity?

One trap, very seductive because of the psychological preoccupation of our times, involves the giving of excessive attention to the cultivating of personal human relationships. Charity comes from God. It is a gift to be prayed for and then accepted with humility of heart, not just a personal achievement to ensure human support and acceptance. Exclusive focus on human relationships becomes dead-end. Some of us may need special help. A psychological counselor can offer us great assistance in understanding some of our feelings, reactions or drives and may suggest ways of handling human situations more gracefully and fruitfully. Ultimately, we want to keep in the forefront the transcendent origin and foundation for Christian charity. If our whole life seems to revolve around the craving for friendship, we may repeatedly experience fits of intense envy or jealousy and then slip into deep depression when our efforts at friendship are rebuffed. We need to find truly transcendent love or we will slip into serious inconsistencies: the ignoring of the transcendent nature of our vocational call and the

[1] Cf. John Cassian, *The Conferences*, Part II, chapter 2.

over-reliance on more tangible sources of human support and security in life.

A second pitfall may be the opposite tendency to enter into excessive and consistent withdrawal from our peers. Initially, we may have been attracted to a life which calls for some separation from the patterns of the world because of some unhealthy reasons. We may find little difficulty with structures which call for quiet, routinized daily involvements and external conformity. We may be shy, obedient, cooperative, but unable to enter into or sustain much ordinary intimacy in human relationships. The veneer of cooperative obedience may crumble into rigid stubbornness once the pattern is surfaced and confronted by a director. If we can relax in prayer and enter into an intimate encounter with the living God, this may encourage us to be more open in other areas of life. If these inclinations persist, we may need professional help to handle the wounds which have occasioned such self-protective behavior and to facilitate further emotional development toward more normal relationships.

Sexuality is certainly a live issue in contemporary society and in the Church. Whereas preaching and teaching used to focus more on the dangers or risks in sexual abuse in the past, now either the pulpit is silent in this area or the message seems to focus on the wholesomeness of sexual expression. In truth, sexuality, as a gift from God is truly good. As fallen creatures, however, we experience our own sexuality and the sexuality of others in an ambivalent way: it moves us to go beyond ourselves in attractive care and love for others; it also arouses in us manipulative or seductive drives which feed lustful thoughts and desires. In a later chapter, there will be a more extensive treatment of this sacred area of human experience. Suffice it to state here, that as disciples of the Lord, we cannot make peace with overt genital sexual behavior outside the marriage covenant. And repetitive auto-erotic genital or masturbatory behavior is a symptom which should be explored reverently and humbly to determine its underlying causes and to make appropriate healing possible. Every disciple experiences some disorientation in the sexual area. No one of us is free from disordered desires, feelings, and thoughts; some may experience ambiguity in sexual orientation; few are free from some disordered actions over a lifetime. Some great saints, like Augustine, experienced a long struggle in this area. But we cannot lose sight of the inspired direction we are called to enter upon. In faith, we know that our bodies are temples of the Holy Spirit (1 Cor. 6:9). With God's grace, chaste love is truly possible; it is gift to be prayed for.

Another drive that can place stress on charity is anger. The contemporary period of rapid change and an increased sense of powerlessness over factors beyond individual human control seems to give rise to an extraordinary prevalence of anger: anger at parents, anger at institutions, anger at social, economic and political systems. Anger is rooted in a wholesome aggressive drive which makes initiative possible for creative enterprises, and which can express itself in the face of danger. It also leads to the kind of anger at evil which mobilizes the best in us to struggle resolutely against the powers of evil which tend to engulf the whole world. When anger, however, becomes directed consistently against specific people or institutions to a degree that is disproportionate to any objective wrong inflicted and is not accompanied by any discernible self-insight, it poses a problem for true Christian charity. We want to bring this anger to God, to reflect gently on its causes and to seek healing. If we refuse to face this anger and allow it to rule our daily life, we may find ourselves indulging in angry outbursts, hypercriticism or hostile withdrawal. This kind of behavior suggests the need of expert help because it blocks spiritual growth.

Another significant area of concern is indifference or hostility to the social mission of the Church. We may find ourselves inclined to a more privatized religious practice. As the world shrinks in size through the extraordinary developments in travel and communication, as the population increases, as the harsh inequities among peoples become more manifest, as incidents of oppression multiply, we cannot shy away from a truly expansive concern for the poor. Family background and training may incline us to limited horizons and domestic concerns. It will be important to bring this inner reluctance to God and allow him to touch us with the universally redemptive love which brought him into this world and became expressed in his special love for the poor.

Lastly, an age which seems to have spawned very strained relationships between parents and their children may contribute to some complications in our relationships with authority figures or directors. Our desire to enter into a trustful relationship with authority or a good director may be sidetracked. The capacity to trust an older person can be grievously undermined by the serious disappointments occasioned by some significant adult figures in earlier life. Yet discipleship is deepened by a trusting manifestation of the heart to a spiritual director. This is an especially graced means for entering on the spiritual journey more fruitfully. Ever since the desert fathers discovered the practice, the Church has asked some form of humble self-revelation of those who profess to enter religious life or serve the Church in ordained ministry. The same is important for those who enter into newer church ministries. Normally, a growing facility in self-revelation is very slow in developing. It depends on adequate self-knowledge and the emergence of a humble heart. If, however, we find it impossible or extremely difficult to open up at all to a director, we may be experiencing serious problems in handling intimacy, anger, or trust. We want to move beyond these problems in order to enter serious discipleship.

These are some of the struggles we may encounter on the uneven road to Christian charity. Our growing communion with God, deeper conversion of heart and more expansive life of charity lead us into the heart of the mystery of the Church.

MATURING LOVE FOR THE CHURCH

One of the most moving talks I ever heard from the lips of a student was given by a young man who was about to be ordained a deacon. He was addressing young freshmen in college and shared with them the journey he had travelled in the previous seven years as he tried to face the questions of Church and vocation in his life. He came from a believing family and had entered the seminary college because he thought he wanted to become a priest. But his entrance into the seminary coincided with the beginning of seminary turmoil and confusion in the latter half of the sixties. First seminary, then Church, then faith came under serious attack. Soon he did not know where he stood. His closest friend left the seminary after completing college and became a "seeker." The friend had found some of the social causes supplanting the original purpose that had brought him into the seminary. He had become a loner, a vegetarian and a wanderer. What troubled the would-be deacon most was that his friend seemed so bitter and sad. All of this upset him terribly and catapulted him into a period of extended inner turmoil. He resented the Church and seminary because, in his eyes, they had caused this to happen. Then gradually with the help of a spiritual director and a counselor, he began to face his own inner struggles. He was able to differentiate *his* life's experience, *his* faith and *his* unique vocational call from that of his friend. He began to understand better what had happened to his friend. He gradually came to sense something of the deeper meaning of Church and could see himself as giving his life to serve this Church. He begged his listeners never to look at the Church exclusively from the outside; for, as he said, the church in a broad sense is made up of all who earnestly seek to find the God who initially created them and calls them.

A few years later, I met this same man, ordained a priest and laboring fruitfully in a suburban parish. His father had just died. He expressed how graced he felt himself to be in witnessing how his mother had patiently cared for his father for two years while the father's terminal illness caused him to become extremely cantankerous and impossible to please. He saw in her the faithful living of vowed love which spoke eloquently to him of the power and beauty of sacrificial consecration to vocation.

This man has touched deeper reality in life. He has come to appreciate how tangible things are not all what they initially seem to be . . . and that there is a level of life into which Christ leads his disciples that opens up entirely new vistas. He discovered this especially about the Church. Although a stumbling block to many, the Church is the usual way in which Christ leads his followers to communion with the Father, conversion of heart, and Christian charity.

The sacrament of Christ

Despite all the biblical images of the Church, the fathers at the Vatican Council II seemed to prefer to describe the Church first as the sacrament of Christ (*Lumen gentium,* 1). Just as Christ is the sacrament of God, the Church is the sacrament of Christ and the seven sacramental celebrations are concrete and specially-graced ways in which Christ is present to the Church's members in the course of their lives. This use of the term, sacrament, of course, is not arbitrary. The term is a latinization of the biblical word *mysterion,* meaning a sacred reality, partially revealed, yet partially veiled from the knowledge of man. Certainly in Christ, the sacred reality of the Godhead is partially revealed and partially veiled. So, too, in the Church, the continuing presence of the Risen Lord is partially revealed and partially veiled.

The parallel, however, is not perfect. In Christ's humanity there is a sinless manifestation of God. In the Church's members there is a weak and sinful manifestation of Christ. In approaching the Church, therefore, there is a need to come with a sense of mystery and a capacity to penetrate beyond weak and sinful people, weak and sinful structures and even weak and sinful policies. Only if we have some degree of self-knowledge and a spirit of personal repentance can we accept an imperfect Church with equanimity of heart.

Biblical images

There is no single passage in Sacred Scripture which exhaustively defines or even describes the Church. In fact no mere words could, no matter how inspired they were. But the Scriptures do offer images which capture different aspects of the mystery of the Church.

Like the Jews of old, the followers of Christ became a people born into this new life and relationship with God through baptism in the Lord's death and resurrection. They became the new *People of God* (1 Pt. 2:9). The emphasis here is on the qualifying phrase, "of God." The Church is made up of those of us who have become God's people, been reborn in water and the Spirit, been consecrated to live the Christ-life.

The Church is also described as God's *temple* (1 Cor. 3:16). In the Old Testament, the temple was the sacred place where God dwelt. It was also the place where the Jews offered worship to God. When David had originally planned to build the house for God, God revealed to him through Nathan that it was God who eventually would build him a house through his progeny (2 Sam. 7:5-16). Jesus, the son of David, later claimed he himself was the new temple (Jn. 2:22), because in him God dwelt among men and in him perfect worship was being offered to the Father. Moreover, Jesus promised to his followers that he would remain with them until the end of time (Mt. 28:20) and that they would be able to worship God in spirit and in truth (Jn. 4:23-24). Jesus' continued presence among men is realized in a unique way in the Church and it is the Church that continues to offer true spiritual worship to the Father in Christ Jesus.

The Church's Eucharistic nature is imaged in the parable of the *vine and the branches* (Jn. 15:1-8). John the Evangelist includes this parable in the last supper discourse. The fruit of the vine was on the table and about to be transformed. Jesus revealed to them that they, his closest followers and the nucleus of his Church, had to remain in close union with him if they wished to bear fruit. He was the vine. They were the branches. If they wished to bear fruit, they would have to undergo pruning. Whatever they tried to do, it was important to remember that they could not bear fruit for the kingdom except in union with him. In this context, John suggests that Jesus explained the deeper nature of the call to Christian charity in the Church and then proceeded to transform the fruit of the vine into his own blood.

Another rich dimension of the Church is revealed in the spousal image (Eph. 5:29). The Church is a *virgin spouse* of Christ invited into a mystical marriage with the Lord. This theme has prompted a number of spiritual writers, beginning with Origen, to draw on the Old Covenant marital imagery to express the intimacy offered by God to the human soul. Just as spiritual commentaries on the Our Father became normative to instruct people in the fundamentals of prayer, so spiritual commentaries on the Song of Songs provided the occasion for instruction on mystical prayer and love. God binds himself to man in a sacred, intimate covenant in the Church.

Paul developed at some length his inspired understanding of the Church as the *body of Christ*. He understood from the time of his conversion experience that Christ was identified in his risen body with his disciples (Acts 9:4). He taught that Christians are bodily united with the risen body of the Lord (Rm.8:11) by baptism (1 Cor. 12:13) and the Eucharist (1 Cor. 10:16). Thus, they become part of Christ's body (1 Cor. 6:15) united in such a way that Christ and the disciples together form the Body of Christ (1 Cor.12:27). This Body is the Church (Eph.1:22; Col.1:18), made one in the one Spirit (Eph.4:4). Christ is the head of this Body (Eph. 1:22). Each of the members of the Church has his own gift for the upbuilding of the Body (1 Cor.12:27-30).

Each of these images sheds some limited light on the many-splendored mystery of the Church. The Church is the sacrament of Christ's continuing presence on earth. It is composed of people reborn to new life in Christ Jesus. This life is a real share in Christ's life, making it possible to worship the Father in spirit and in truth. We Christians continue to experience this life insofar as we remain in union with Christ. This union with Christ is open to mystical intimacy in prayer and life. In fact, it involves a kind of union of all Christians with Christ's risen body effecting one perduring Body of Christ, with Christ as the head and all Christians as members. Each of us has a unique function to perform for the good of the whole.

In addition to these images which directly refer to the Church, the Scriptures report that Jesus spoke frequently of the kingdom of God. He uttered the parable of the sower (Mt. 13:4-9), the darnel (Mt. 13:24-30), the mustard seed (Mt. 13:31-32), the yeast (Mt. 13:33), the treasure in the field and the pearl of great price (Mt. 13:44-46) and the dragnet (Mt. 13:47-50). These offer insights into the kingdom which most scholars consider to include more than the Church. But these same images also reveal truths which in an analogous sense apply to the Church as well: the Church is the place where God's word is sown with varying results; in the Church, saints and sinners grow up side by side; the saving mystery of redemption emerges from small insignificant beginnings and embraces large numbers of people; the source of life, although hidden, bears rich fruit; the riches entrusted to the Church are worth trading all that a person has to gain; the Church includes all kinds of people whose true worth will only be known on the last day.

The Church, then, is a multi-faceted mystery. Yet for all its richness, the Church continues to be a stumbling block for some of us.

The call to be ecclesial Christians

Probably the least attractive image which describes part of the Church's life is *institution.* The Church is truly an institution with many of the characteristics which mark the life of human institutions: authority, order, laws, courts, offices of administration, a diversity of official services, financial needs, public policies. Moreover, it also suffers from the debilitating liabilities of all human institutions: heavy bureaucracy, incompetence, factionalism, defensiveness, some moral paralysis or social myopia. It is the institutional dimension of the Church that often draws most attention.

How can we become ecclesial people without becoming either ecclesiastical parasites or disillusioned ecclesiastical cynics? Is it possible to become more and more Church without becoming churchy? Is it possible to resist churchiness without becoming Church rebels?

The first step toward sound ecclesial spirituality is taken when we, like the young man mentioned at the beginning of this chapter, truly appreciate that we are the Church in a real, although incomplete sense. The Church is not the clergy alone; nor is it a people of God distinct from ourselves. Just as every parish is a microsm of the universal

Church, so we, in an imperfect way, are the Church in miniature. Just as we experience limitation and weakness in our own body, so the Church is a finite organism. Just as we know within ourselves the capacity for and the reality of sin, so the Church is both capable of sin and in need of continual renewal because of sin. This step toward ecclesial spirituality is rooted in the kind of personal conversion of life which leads to greater humility before God, patience with ourselves and genuine compassion for others.

Difficulties along the way

One of the strongest obstacles to this kind of ecclesial conversion can be perfectionism. Often those of us who offer ourselves for Church ministry have a very strong desire to be perfect. Instead of understanding the Matthean text which records Jesus' invitation to be perfect as the Heavenly Father is perfect (Mt.5:48) in the way that the original language expresses it, we are sometimes inclined to try to be literally perfect in every detail of our lives. The word, "perfect," actually means to be moving toward one's goal, to be fulfilling one's purpose. This call invites us into a gradual process of response. Instead of a humble, patient, compassionate movement toward the invitations God issues, the perfectionist has a tendency to repress certain areas of his own weakness, to become angry in the face of failure and to judge moral imperfection or sin quite harshly. Jesus was very strong in exposing this folly of pharisaeism. It blinds its adherents to their own need for redemption and to deeper realities that are so freeing.

Another difficulty we may face takes the form of ambivalent attitudes toward the institution of the Church. These attitudes may be rooted in dubious parental affection experienced in early life. Smothering or controlling parental care can engender both a dependence on a strong institutional role in life and yet a festering resentment of the unfreedom this causes. This can lead to a love-hate experience: an instinctive attraction to strong ecclesiastical life, yet a persistent cynicism or hyper-criticism of Church leaders. This kind of immaturity causes tremendous harm to the Church and to true faith. For if it persists, it diverts other people from true religion. Neurotic religious practice alienates some people from the true Church and prevents others from finding it. This is the kind of behavior that incurred the wrath of Jesus: "Alas for you, scribes and Pharisees, you hypocrites! You who shut up the kingdom of heaven in men's faces, neither going in yourselves nor allowing others to go in who want to" (Mt. 23:13).

In its most unattractive form, this passive-dependent approach to life and religion is expressed in ecclesiastical narcissism. The failure to grow beyond passive dependence usually leads to a paralyzing love for the false self. In return for the generous gesture of giving our life to the

Church, we may begin to expect the Church to serve our every need. This emotional immaturity then moves toward moral selfishness. In the seminarian or priest, it is often called clericalism. But in all Church people it leads to a demanding, manipulative, self-serving pattern of life. Paradoxically, the very transcendent commitments regarding things, people, and events which the evangelical virtues express and which all disciples profess to embrace in some way, become subverted into the craving to receive the best of this world's power, glory or goods, to possess other people in manipulative friendship and to conspire so that decisions and events suit our own ends.

It is difficult to face this pattern in ourselves without help. We need good, competent spiritual direction, even though we will probably be inclined to keep our distance from a strong director. If we sense that a director can be manipulated, we will be tempted to take advantage of this. We may consciously, or more likely unconsciously, play to the needs of this more vulnerable director and form a friendship which really avoids the central issue. If on the other hand, a good director faces us with our need for growth, we may be inclined to respond very angrily or we may go through the motions of accepting the comments during the conversation and then criticize the director strongly with our peers. We need a director who can remain firm and kindly while resisting the bait for open hostility or angry rejection. If the roots of this difficulty are in the unconscious, we will probably need extended therapy to move beyond this kind of narcissistic attitude.

One of the unfortunate by-products of unfaced narcissistic inclinations can be a resistance to any ecumenical ministry. Even without clarifying the distinction between genuine ecumenism and doctrinal indifferentism, we can find ourselves callously dismissing the urgency of ecumenical collaboration. The more immature we are, the more difficulty we will have reaching beyond our own limited horizons and unredeemed patterns of life. The zealous heart, however, is eager to recognize and strengthen the elements of true faith and life wherever they are found. The redemptive heart is pained by division and scandalized by hostilities occasioned by misplaced religious loyalties.

Another strong obstacle to ecclesial conversion is the more adolescent struggle which seeks independence from persons who tend to control our life. In many ways, it is a sign of greater maturity than the narcissistic patterns just described. In fact, it may only be a passing phase indicating growth toward wholesome adulthood. We will want to accept help to facilitate this growth toward responsible interdependence.

One way this inclination may manifest itself is in the desire to be totally free of supervision in life. We may have come from a tightly ruled home. Or, on the other hand, we may have lived in an environment which made a cult of personal rights and freedom. In either case, we have a tendency to test people who are in authority. In facing this tendency, we will probably want to clarify the roots of our attitude and then adjust our approach accordingly. In the first instance, if we have never worked through the transition from a strict home life, we may have to enjoy some room for experimentation. In the second, if we have come from a more liberal background, we may have to discover the differences between external freedom of choice and inner freedom. In any case, we will want to grow into a healthier collaboratie relationship to authority in our lives.

This adolescent spirit will often surface in conflicts over the interpretation of Church disciplinary laws or decisions made by people in authority. Although most norms are considerably liberalized and generalized in the post-Vatican II period, still there will be prescriptions or proscriptions which some of us will inevitably find restrictive. The natural impulse in contemporary society is to negotiate a change in the law. Presuming that the law reflects a reasonably adequate adaptation of the Church's expectations to the local situation, it is good for us to move beyond the impulse to adjust expectations to conform to our own desires every time this happens. There is a wholesome chastening experienced when we accept some restriction that has not been of our own choosing. It opens up a greater possibility of appreciating that freedom of choice is not the same as inner freedom from enslaving impusive and compulsive drives. A director will be able to assist us to discover this truth better by leading us to address our inner resistances on the right level. This should diminish the amount of time and energy consumed in haggling over the interpretation of Church norms or the decisions made by rightful authority.

Occasionally the freedom-struggle will arise in connection with personal conflicts between community concerns and individual desires. Often the individual desire seems far more important than the community concern. Sometimes this will be objectively true and we should recognize this. But, ordinarily, there should be a growing willingness to participate in a life which is larger than our own and will often call for the subjection of personal whim to a wider and deeper life shared in the Church. The mutual support that we give one another is embracing the sacrifice involved in our Church life, our common worship and our service to one another has a very strengthening power.

Probably the greatest challenge in becoming ecclesial Christians is developing enough love for the Church that we want to give ourselves for its continuing life. Love for the Church cannot be passive or complacent. It calls forth the noblest desires for humble self-giving. Paul teaches that "Christ loved the Church and sacrificed himself for her to make her holy" (Eph. 5:25).

We, too, are called to a consecrated love for the Church. We are invited to share in Christ's redemptive love for those people for whom Christ calls us to live. The call to Church ministry is only secondarily a call to serve. It is primarily a call to redemptive love in Christ for the sake of the Church to be expressed in ministry. This is especially clear for the ordained priest who by sacrament is configured to Christ's life and love and challenged to live what he has become in sacrament. In an analogous way, all Christians are invited to recognize the same truth. By baptism, they are incorporated into Christ's life and love. Any work they enter into in life should become an expression of that life and love already maturing in them. Religious draw special attention to this truth. Their primary consecration is to vowed love and the search for holiness of life. Any particular apostolic ministry they may undertake is secondary to that.

Love for the Church has to be sacrificial. It can take a great deal of courage to foster renewal in the Church. History reveals that the Church has been more kind to reformers after their deaths than during their lives. Those that have borne fruit and won such recognition have persevered in their unwavering dedication to the Church even when significant people in the Church have tried to thwart their efforts or to discredit their integrity. Often the experience of adversity has been the occasion for purifying their motivation and deepening their consecration. Obviously, weak people do not develop this type of love. We will want to discover the right kind of prophetic witness. Such witness flows from a humble heart, an almost reluctant attitude toward assuming the role and a strong, even heroic love. It is a gift given to the few, but to be respected by all.

Love for the Church cannot be fragile. It involves a willingness to embrace at least some suffering in living out a consecrated love in the Church (Col. 1:24). The Church does not need us in leadership roles if we are so weak that we break when ordinary adversity enters our lives. Hence, we have to be willing to accept a training that demands sacrifice and challenges self-will. The goal is to develop an inner strength that makes the love for the Church both courageous and realistic.

In sum, the road to true ecclesial life is a rocky and uneven one. But its importance is central. The need at the present time for truly ecclesial men and women is great indeed. The Church cannot risk increasing the number of immature leaders. The immature attract the immature. It is difficult sometimes to become truly ecclesial. So often, we are tempted to see it as a kind of artificial loyalty which bureaucratic institutions tend to encourage. But the real men and women of the Church have touched the deeper truth behind the Scriptures and the tradition, the deeper reality within the sacramental mysteries and the deeper ministry involved in pastoral care. They have entered into a life of sacrificial charity because they find themselves mediating between the life-giving truth which they contemplate and strive to live and the complex pastoral situations in which people inevitably find themselves in life.

If we, then, enjoy some communion with God, have entered into some personal conversion of heart, are growing in Christian charity and maturing in this kind of love for the Church, we are in a graced position to discern before God our vocation in the Church.

CLARIFYING VOCATION IN LIFE

Personal vocational decisions have certainly become increasingly more complex, especially in the western free world. In this post-Vatican II period, many hours of personal reflection and spiritual direction or counseling have been consumed in trying to clarify vocational calls. Individuals who have been living in a state of life for years have suddenly found the supports that had previously strengthened them in an unquestioning approach to their life disintegrating. We have seen the marriages of good people strained beyond the breaking point and then terminated in separation, divorce, remarriage. We know some religious who had entered their consecrated lives with the conviction that they were inwardly free and knew what they were doing and have since been thrown into devastating turmoil as they discovered how inadequately they had entered into living a commitment to the poor, how little they had known about their own sexuality and how immature had been their approach to living with others under a superior. We are familiar with some priests who had entered their ordained ministry in a pre-Vatican II Church and then suddenly sensed that many of the patterns and norms which previously governed their lives and ministry have been significantly changed.

If this has been true for those who had already made permanent commitments in life, it has also been a cause of considerable anxiety in the lives of young people *preparing* to make a commitment. How do we really know our vocation? Is it advisable to experience many different possibilities before making a choice? Do we have to have fully lived the walk of life before we can be sure? Is it really possible to make a permanent commitment in this age of "future shock?" These are some of the questions that have consumed extended moments of personal dialogue and open discussion in many quarters of the Church.

Events have happened so quickly and so many individuals have changed life commitments that we can become seriously shaken in our convictions. As we face the challenges of Church renewal, we may sometimes find our attention drawn more to discontinuity than to continuity. We can begin to regard stability as reactionary or as reflective of an overly rigid temperament. We can dismiss fidelity as often the grim determination to suffer things out to the end, no matter what the human cost. We can regard as creative and optimistic those who claim that the Spirit draws us in dramatically new and untried ways in life vocations.

Those of us who have already entered on a life commitment have had to look humbly and realistically at our original consecration, take the reflective time to recognize both the grace and the sin of our life history and then come to appreciate the contemporary radical questioning in a graced way. For the raising of basic questions introduces much darkness even as it offers a faint new light. The darkness can be terribly frightening and can lead us in panic to conclude that most of our past life has been wasted. The faint new light is the glimmer of God's grace drawing us onward to deeper faith and vision. We have had to let decisions emerge slowly, only after we have lived with the darkness in humility, patience, and faith. The change in pastoral practice on annulments and dispensations has come from the Church's desire to trust more our own sincere discernment. Thus the testimony of the petitioner who claims lack of sufficient freedom or psychological deficiency at the time of the original commitment is more readily accepted. However, juridical statements of annulment or dispensation, like the juridical expression of the original commitments, do not of themselves exonerate us of honest self-confrontation with our living God. The canonical processes govern the external regulation of a life that touches the *whole* person. Undoubtedly, some have left for the wrong reasons; some have stayed for the wrong reasons. It is too early yet to test the fruits of this recent pastoral practice.

A more difficult challenge has faced those who have been preparing to make an initial vocational decision. The atmosphere of live debate in the Church over the indissolubility of marriage, the need for permanency, the appropriateness of mandatory celibacy for diocesan priests, and even the wisdom of vows for religious has been so pervasive. Many have experienced tremendous anxiety about approaching any commitments whatsoever. Some have been more inclined to want to postpone decisions or to talk about trial marriages and five- or ten-year plans in priestly or religious life. This kind of agitated environment has made personal, in-depth reflection and decisions extremely elusive. Some of the decisions made in this atmosphere lacked depth. Some individuals could not come to any decision. But those who had the inner strength to approach their vocational decision humbly and with help are the stronger for their courage and honesty in a difficult time. How, then, should we now approach the road to initial vocational decision?

Desire for God

Spiritual writers have consistently taught that the discipleship of the Lord begins with a real desire for God. It seems so simple and so obvious. Yet, fallen human nature has a way of being diverted from this fundamental starting point. In the baptismal liturgy, the Church asks us: "What do you ask of the Church of God?" The response that is expected is: "Faith." We might spell it out further and say: "Faith *in*

God" or merely, "God." This challenging question the Church continually asks each year at Easter. It is a question that probes the heart. It is an echo of the question which Jesus raised for Andrew and John: "What are you looking for?" (Jn. 1:38).

We do well to keep this question in the forefront as we seek to know our own vocation. Each time we allow ourselves to hear this question, we have to answer it more realistically as we recognize how limited is our response at any one time in our life. It is a question that promotes interiority in that it probes the desires which are deep within the heart. It is also a question that promotes inner freedom because it tends to surface the conflicting and enslaving desires which otherwise can suffocate the deeper desire and thus diminish human freedom.

The growing awareness that our deepest desire is for God helps us to place many other considerations in perspective. The compulsive desires to achieve and the impulsive desires to gratify ourselves become more clear. As a result there is an increasing awareness of the need for some kind of curtailment of more superficial gratifications in order that the more central desires may grow in strength and influence. This is why the spiritual tradition consistently points to the need for mortification and silence. Uncontrolled self-gratification and incessant chatter tend to keep us on a very superficial level of human experience. Balanced mortification and reflective silence, on the other hand, can open up deeper levels of living for us.

A sense of vocation

It is only after the genuine desire for God has come alive and the willingness to forego what may stand in the way of responding to God has been strengthened, that a sense of inner vocation becomes clearer. The search to find one's vocation can be quite frustrating unless these two prior conditions are being met. Unclarified and undisciplined desires lead to conflict and confusion over vocational call. When this inner turmoil is brought face to face with a growing number of real options in an affluent society, the experience can be overwhelming. Some prefer to take refuge in delaying commitment indefinitely.

It may help those who are trying to make an initial vocational decision to recognize that vocational call is experienced on at least three levels of life:[1] first, on an inner unique level in which God invites us to holiness of life; that is, to enter into intimacy with him within the framework of the concrete circumstances of our life; secondly, in a basic state of life, such as marriage, religious life, priesthood or celibate life in the world; thirdly, in specific occupational tasks. The first is of

[1]Cf. Adrian van Kaam, *In Search of Spiritual Identity*. (Denville, N.J.: Dimension Books, 1975), pp. 138-171 for an excellent exposition of these levels of vocational call.

primary importance; the second of great importance; the third of least importance. Because the differences in these levels of vocational call are rarely understood, it may be helpful to dwell on them briefly.

The most fundamental vocational call touches the inner core of our being and suggests the way that we are being called to live with God in our heart and in the world. This is the level that is least understood because it seems more vague and elusive. Perhaps an example may help.

Recently, a young woman in her early twenties, a medical assistant, sat beside me on a plane trip between two western cities. She had just flown to the coast to interview for a job as an airline stewardess. But she was very discouraged because she felt sure that the interview had not gone well. While she was out there, she visited and bade farewell to a school chum who was about to enter a cloistered contemplative monastery. This had tripped her memory of some of her own earlier fantasies about becoming a missionary. This idea she had long since let slip into the background. Very serious illness had interrupted her college education. In fact, the sickness had been so severe that she had not been expected to live. In a vague, but real way, she sensed that God had rescued her from the jaws of death.

As she continued to talk, some things struck me very forcibly. First, she had a real desire to discover what God wanted of her in life. In addition, she had a real love for people. She had a very gracious smile and obviously cared about others in the sensitivity she manifested to those around her. She seemed to want to enter into *deeper* relationships with people because she had spoken of the possibility of wearing a cross as an airline stewardess in the hope that it might invite conversation about Jesus Christ. She also had a great deal of anxiety about choosing the right life work. She wanted to make sure it was pleasing to God. In the conversation, I commented to her about her desire for God, her gracious and sensitive love for people, her attraction to entering into deeper service to people. She was visibly moved. I suggested to her that her choice of a state in life and a life work was secondary to being true to that *inner* call. What was important was fidelity to that inner call whatever she did or wherever she went. Obviously, God wanted to lead her to choose a state in life and an occupation which were as consonant with that call as possible. But such decisions had to be made in dialogue with the real concrete possibilities in her life. The inner call did not necessarily mean missionary life or marriage; it did not point indisputably to medical or airline service. What was paramount, was the response in her heart to the inner call and her living it out faithfully in whatever state she embraced in life. At the end of our journey, she insisted on introducing me to her boyfriend who had come to meet her and then embraced me in silence. Her whole being resonated a sense of inner silence, bespeaking the calm and peace that seemed to have graced her heart.

Our conversation had moved ultimately to the primary and fundamental call which can place all other decisions in perspective. Only God knows the ultimate meaning and value of this exchange just described. But, perhaps recounting the incident does help to clarify an understanding of this first level of vocational call. If we can focus attention on this level, we can allow the decision on other levels to fall into place. Often our attention can become riveted on the vocational *state* in life. If this happens, then one of two things can follow: we may blindly focus on a particular state of life as our life call and cling to it no matter what the real signs may suggest; or we may experience extraordinary anxiety about making a life-long decision when the evidence is not that clear nor the future that predictable. The first results in our claiming a "right" to be married immediately or be ordained or be allowed to enter Church ministry or make religious profession because we claim to know for certain that God is calling us even when there are serious objections. The second leads to existential paralysis, an inability to make personal decisions involving commitment. It is ths fundamental level of vocational call that invites us to want to live in union with God in any circumstance, thus taking the pressure off the decision on the vocational state in life. In greater peace and receptivity of heart, we then can beg God to reveal to us his will for all other areas of our life.

These considerations should help to make more clear the different nature of the second level of vocation: a state in life. The number of basic states in life is limited: married life and celibate life. Obviously, married life involves as many further choices as available marital partners may allow. Celibate life may be lived in a religious community or in the secular sphere. Religious life includes a monastic life, a mendicant life, or active religious life with all of the various orders, congregations and houses, lay and clerical. The celibate life in the world includes diocesan priesthood, lay institutes and the vast variety of individual celibate lives open to us. But, in effect, the principal vocational decision on a state of life revolves around married life, religious life, and secular celibate life.

Choice of the most appropriate state of life is quite important, but not of ultimate importance. If an understanding of the more fundamental vocational call to holiness is missed, inordinate attention can be focused on the choice of a state in life. Until the advent of the modern period in first and second world culture, people did not experience much freedom with regard to marriage (including the choice of partner) and even religious life (young boys and girls would sometimes be given over to communities at a very early age) and secular celibate life (usually, this was the result of not being able to enter into either of the first two states.) In some areas of the third world, free choice in these areas is still quite limited. The emergence of free choice is obviously a great development even though it brings mixed blessings. It encourages much more personal and deep involvement in our state of life. But it also arouses in us extraordinary anxiety about making the right choice of a state in life and inclines us to invest unrealistic expectations for fulfillment from the living of this life choice. We begin to feel that happiness will depend almost exclusively on the right choice. The prevalence of unhappiness in individuals' lives seems to suggest to the young that the chances of success are slim. Hence, the pressure to enter states of life on a trial basis (pre-marital sexual experimentation, living together without benefit of marriage, "temporary" vocations to the priesthood and religious life.) Hence, also, the almost desperate search for another chance when some serious unhappiness is encountered—for example, the growing pervasiveness of divorce and remarriage, serial marriages and the movement from celibate life to marriage.

Certainly there is something very wrong in this kind of social pressure. It supplants the tight parental or ecclesiastical control of the past with a more subtle yet real enslavement to unrealistic expectations about the happiness we should experience in our state of life. Frustrated expectations lead to anger, resentment, open, even violent hostility and depression. Certainly these unfortunate results abound in our contemporary society.

If, on the other hand, attention can be drawn to the more fundamental vocational call to holiness described above, some of the unreal expectations invested in life choice can be diminished. Real happiness revolves around an inner response to the way in which God is revealing his face to us in daily life no matter what the state of life. Circumstances beyond control have led a number of people into a particular life choice that produces considerable hardship. If we immediately begin to feel we have made a mistake in our life decision, our attempts to address the situation become seriously undermined. Instead of recognizing the hand of God in adversity, instead of marshaling resources to respond creatively and responsibly to the challenge, instead of being moved to humble repentance for any personal fault in the difficulty, instead of perceiving God's purifying call to greater depth, the inclination is to seek a way out, an alternate way to find the Promised Land. In some instances, a change of state of life may be called for. But it is, then, a change made very reluctantly in order to be more faithful to the inner-life call.

God's invitation is to *try* to enter into the vocational state that is most consonant with the interior call. The decision has to be made within the framework of the real possibilities. Other trusted people are usually involved in testing this decision. Then we move ahead, in faith and humility of heart, confident that God is with us in the inner call and that God has pledged to be faithful to us in our vocational state no matter what trials emerge later on.

Finally, the commitment to occupational work falls into place. The

A Practical Guide To Spiritual Formation

vocation to a particular kind of professional work is subordinate not only to the inner vocational call, but also to the state of life. There is much more room for experimentation here. It may be that the experience in one type of work has not worked out well. Wisdom may suggest a career change. Even more so than in the state of life, it is important to refrain from investing our hopes for happiness exclusively in our work. Our work, especially if it is professional, can become wholly absorbing. But it is not God. It should not compete with family, religious community or celibate consecration. Nor should it ever squeeze out the unique relationship with God that is so central.

Thus the airplane companion described above may find that her most fundamental call is to an intimacy with God, grounded in a realization that God not only has created her, but has also shown special providential care in saving her from death. This intimate call, moreover, may lead her to personal, in-depth care and concern for the health and holiness of others. On the second level, she may eventually marry her boyfriend and live out this inner call to holiness in relation to her husband and their children as well as with friends. On the third level, she may temporarily enter into a career as an airline stewardess or she may remain as a medical assistant, attempting to translate her inner call into some concrete ways of life within those careers. Or, on both the second and third levels, she may one day discover that her inner call can be lived out more appropriately as a medical missionary sister. But these decisions on her state in life and on her career should now be more manageable. She need not invest all her hopes and expectations for happiness in them alone. Hopefully, she has come to recognize that the unique faithful love God has for her in Christ Jesus is deeper and broader than that.

Vocation within the Church

Greater appreciation of this sense of inner vocation to intimate relationship with God is one of the great needs of our times. It can help to restore a sense of the holiness of marriage, bring greater stability to family life and lead both religious and priests to a deeper level of life. For, as we realize that we have this unique call to intimacy with God that preceeds and undergirds the vocational decision, we may be more able to recognize that every walk of life involves a calling from God. There is no walk of life which is of itself more holy than another. Holiness is rooted in the degree of love of God and neighbor which pervades the way we live our life calling. Consecrated religious, by their calling, are expected to remind us all of this truth.

This inner sense of vocational call to experience a closeness with God and a holiness of life impels us to want to live out all the areas of our life for God. Thus it becomes the basis for receiving another kind of grace, the gift of our state in life. This second grace is offered in a special way for the sake of the whole body of Christ: "Just as each of our bodies has several parts and each part has a special function, so all of us, in union with Christ, form one body, and as parts of it, we belong to each other. Our gifts differ according to the grace given us" (Rm. 12:4-6).

That is why the Church has understood that Christ's intention was first to call all to holiness and then to establish certain basic states in life as special vehicles of grace to others. Thus marriage and orders—the diaconate, priesthood, and episcopate—are sacramental states for the upbuilding of the Body. Religious vows and virginal consecration are recognized publicly, not only as sources of grace for those involved, but also for the Church as a whole.

In this sense, every state of life involves a gift given to us for the Church. This is true in a unique way of ordained life because the sacrament of orders configures a man to Christ's role in the depths of his being and consecrates him to public proclamation of the word, public celebration of the sacramental realities and a public pastoral ministry of charity in the Church. No one can presume to assume that his inner desire to be a priest is God's call. It must be brought to the Church and tested with those designated for this role, both in the external forum and the internal forum of conscience. In a special way, the priestly role will, then, provide the ordinary means for others to test and clarify *their* role in the Church. Vocational discernment is not merely subjective or interior. Although each one's gift is directly from God, it is to be ordered and sanctified by God through those publicly committed to Holy Order.

Although there is an essential difference in the sacramentally-rooted ministry of the ordained priest, all Christians are invited to a ministry in the Church in a broad sense. The primary ministry of the lay person is the apostolate in the secular arena. Every Christian's task in the world can become redemptive if entered into in union with Christ's saving mission. This is real lay ministry. Some, however, may be called to temporary and part-time service in liturgy, public lectoring, music or teaching. Others may be invited to a full-time service of pastoral care. Married persons who enter Church ministry have to respect their primary commitment to marriage and family. This is especially true for married permanent deacons. All who enter an explicit Church ministry are expected to work in a complementary way, respecting the graced role of holy order in uniting the charisms for the building of Christ's body. Those in orders, for their part, are expected truly to foster and encourage the variety of gifts of the Spirit in the Church.

An initial decision for Church ministry

In making an initial commitment for Church ministry, we want to listen attentively to what Church leaders ask. The obvious requirements are generally made clear during a training program. But other expectations are more interior. First, the Church expects a reasonable human maturity of its potential leaders. Although God can work through anyone he chooses, he usually grants his grace of leadership to those who already have a sound human potential: emotional, intellectual, and moral. Grace ordinarily builds on nature. So concerned is the Holy See[2] about this that bishops are asked to use every human means, including psychological testing, to ensure that there is basic maturity in our future leaders.

Secondly, the Church asks a sincere desire for union with God and an honest conviction that God may very well be inviting us to live out our inner call to holiness in this particular ministry. The desire for God, however undeveloped it may be, is very important. If we have not found this desire in our heart, then the chances are that the wrong reasons for presenting ourselves for ministry will predominate. It is one thing to enter a ministry training program or seminary or novitiate for motives which later are recognized as peripheral to the life. It is another thing to make the more formal initial commitment on this same basis. Motivation is always ambiguous, a mixture of good and bad. But there should be some beginning awakening of a sincere desire to love God wherever he may lead.

We need to be humble enough to present ourselves as we truly see ourselves so as to test both our maturity and the authenticity of our desire for God. Obviously there will be weaknesses which we will want to continue to address in our further preparation. But a basic human maturity and a sincere desire for God are indispensable. We will want to grow in a capacity to accept the reality that we merely present ourselves and ask the Church to make a judgment through those designated.

Similar to, but not synonymous with this desire for God is the inner sense of the call to holiness within a Church ministry. If we, for instance, only see a particular Church ministry as an intriguing career which offers many possibilities for the exercise of our gifts, we have not yet grown to sense an interior call to this walk of life. Full-time lay pastoral ministry, diaconate, priesthood and apostolic religious life are not primarily careers. They require an interior sense of call to enable us to continue to grow in the life in the midst of adversity. So, if we have not yet moved beyond self-serving reasons, we are not yet ready for the initial commitment. We may still be knocking at the door, but we have not really entered.

Some of us discover that we first contemplated a particular Church ministry because we thought that this was the *only* way we could serve God. As the richness of the various calls in the Church becomes known

[2]Cf. Sacred Congregation for Catholic Education, *A Guide to Formation in Priestly Celibacy* (Washington, D.C.: USCC Publications, 1974), pp. 20-31; 35-36.

and a clearer understanding of what is specifically true of the particular ministry we have tentatively entered emerges, then we may begin to lose our enthusism for the life we have provisionally entered. This can be a great grace inviting us to a holy life in another vocational state. That is one of the reasons why the Church insists on a special period of preparation.

Finally, we want to be particularly careful that we are not moving along to an initial decision primarily because our friends are doing the same. We may not yet have personalized our own decision. We see no over-powering reason to refrain from this commitment. Yet, we have not uncovered the inner deeper motivation. We may even experience a vague anxiety about the possibility of having to start anew some place else in our competitive world if we were to decide against the life. Or, we may sense some uneasiness about other options. So we prefer to continue on rather than explore the meaning of this anxiety. This kind of motivation is more negative than positive and insufficient for such a step.

In making these decisions, a spiritual director is so very helpful. If we can find a director who is a deep believer and is competnt in helping us discern inner movements of our heart, we will have received a great gift. We need help in answering the call of faith; we need help in facing the obstacles in ourselves. A humble, faith-filled, strong, but gentle director can fulfill the Baptist's role of guiding disciples with true potential for leadership to the Lord Jesus.

Gradual growth in vocational response

Usually it is only in retrospect that we appreciate more fully that our decision to enter a particular state of life has been in response to an inner call. The factors that initially attract and move us toward exploring a life calling are not usually so noble and exalted. In fact, quite peripheral factors may exercise considerable influence in the beginning. For instance, the external charm of a potential marriage partner or the personal magnetism of a particularly attractive priest or fascination with a distinctive religious garb may play a prominent role at the start. We may even be attracted by less healthy reasons. No one's initial motivation is completely admirable. But experience reveals that God can use absolutely any reason as his initial bait.

Usually, we need the help of others in moving beyond the first motivation. Eventually, we will find that our first motives were quite immature. When this begins to happen, we will want to look back with the appreciation of prayerful faith to see God's hand and then to explore deeper motivation that might make continuing in the life a more mature choice. Motivation should never be analyzed harshly. Rather, the best approach is to bring the motives of which we are conscious to

God's loving and purifying gaze. This helps us to move forward in continuity with our past.

There is always a real danger that the progress of vocational life may be side-tracked by making an idol out of a person, an institute, a way of life or a social cause.[3] Part of the journey in faith involved here is a search for a more authentic relationship with God. But that is really more of a gift given than a goal that is achieved. Hence, human impatience can prompt us to substitute a more tangible object of affection. Our preoccupation with a noble friendship or task or cause can take the place of the true worship of a transcendent God. This is why our entrance into personal presence to the transcendent is so central in spiritual initiation.

If this pursuit of an intermediate good perdures, it will lead to much unhappiness. Our horizons will be limited, if not suffocating. When the full realization of what we are doing strikes us, we can feel quite disillusioned. This rude awakening can catapult us into real hatred for the very person or group or cause we previously worshipped.

Sometimes this crisis surfaces in mid-life. We may have lived what we have reason to believe is about half our expected life-span. Achievement has been moderate. Other people have ceased to applaud us. Young people take us for granted and may test themselves by baiting us. We may sense some of the real emotional, social, intellectual or spiritual underdevelopment in our lives. We are seriously tempted to consider other life alternatives which have the aura of more potential fulfillment. Classical literature is replete with stories of people who in mid-life came to realize that much of the way they had been living their lives was inauthentic and who are subsequently attracted to flirt with another love. Heroic figures suffer through this crisis in a purifying way and emerge better people because of it. Tragic figures succumb in the face of this crisis. Their suffering seems to destroy rather than to redeem them.

Permanent commitment

Because of the prevalence of what seem to be tragic figures in the living of life-long commitment, many today profess skepticism about our ability to enter into them. Some professionals will confess that psychologically speaking, it is not possible to make a permanent commitment. It is true that we do not know ourselves with certainty to anyone or anything. It can only be done in faith.

Edward Farrell, in his book, *Disciples and Other Strangers,* relates a conversation he had with a young woman who was about to make final vows in a religious community. He asked her if she had any misgivings

[3]Adrian van Kaam, *Religion and Personality* (Englewoods Cliffs, N.J.: Prentice-Hall, 1964), pp. 120-131.

about such a consecration in an age when so many seemed to be abandoning it. Her response was: "I would be sad if my God did not love me enough to ask me to give him everything. He loves me; I love him. Isn't that enough?"[4]

This incident puts life-commitment in its proper perspective. The initiative comes from God as personally experienced in his love. Thus, the consecration to one state of life is merely a human response to God's personal self-giving, freely offered. The expectation of being able to live out this consecration is rooted in Christian faith and hope. God has pledged his fidelity, no matter what happens. We are willing, then, to be drawn beyond ourselves to participate more fully in that mystery.

Fortunately, God normally calls when we are young and our weaknesses are known only to him. If we were to know all our weakness or focus all our attention on it, we could never make a gift of our whole selves. If, however, we bring our weakness to God, we can be strengthened by him. "For, it is when I am weak that I am strong" (2 Cor. 12:10).

The initial decision on a state of life is important, but not final. Whether it is engagement before marriage or initial commitment in religious life or admission to candidacy before diaconate and priesthood, it introduces us into a period of seriously trying to live many aspects of the life to which we aspire and testing our own inner experience. In entering into this preliminary commitment, we allow ourselves a graced period to explore inner reactions to our proposed life. If we humbly and honestly strive to become aware of these reactions and test them with a competent director, we will clarify more surely the ways God may be leading us. Two factors will be of importance; namely, our attempt to live the provisional commitment *wholeheartedly* will reveal better the inner congruence or incongruence of the life for us; our willingness to keep the primary desire for God central will better enable us to reflect with others on the experience of this life with objectivity and equanimity of heart. This kind of approach to vocational decision helps us accept more readily the ultimate decision the Church may make regarding our desire for Church ministry.

[4]Edward Farrell, *Disciples and Other Strangers* (Denville, N.J.: Dimension Books, 1974), p. 25.

A Practical Guide To Spiritual Formation

PART TWO

CONTINUING ON THE ROAD TO DEPTH
IN CHURCH MINISTRY

Life is a continuum. There cannot be a decisive line of demarcation between the issues that we face in life before and after an initial decision for Church ministry. Moreover, each of us is drawn by God in unique ways. Hence, we will meet issues at varying points along the way. There are, however, some emphases that belong more to one period or the other. Most of the issues to be treated in this second part of the book are further developments of the areas we looked at in preparation for an initial public decision. A more profound involvement in these issues presupposes that we have already entered into some greater communion with God, a deeper personal conversion of heart, a more expansive Christian charity, a more mature love for the Church and a greater assurance that the seed of a Church vocation truly comes from God.

Part II of this book presumes that the reader has made at least an initial public decision for Church ministry. I will use the term *Church ministry* to include all who work in close collaboration with the ordained ministry of word, sacrament, and pastoral care. Besides the ordained ministry of deacons, priests, and bishops, it includes all religious and lay people who offer their gifts and expertise for direct Church service and seek some formal incorporation into the Church's explicit mission. Although it does not include the broader ministry of all lay persons who are called to true redemptive witness in the various areas of secular life, still there will be much in Part II that will also be applicable to their wider life and apostolate.

CONSECRATING SEXUAL LOVE

Sexuality is certainly a preoccupation among people living in contemporary society. Literature, film, drama, business, advertising, psychological theory, counseling and even daily news and conversation seem to focus attention on sexuality. Young people growing up are inclined to talk about it much more freely and unabashedly than in the past. And there certainly is considerable sexual experimentation going on among people of all ages.

In this atmosphere, we cannot proceed very far in preparation for Church ministry before we need to clarify and deepen our appreciation of our own sexuality and that of others. We need a good director with whom we can share our experience and our questions. A good director will be reverent and will facilitate this for us. But before entering into some of the personal issues, it may be wise to acknowledge some of the larger factors which affect our experience of sexuality.

Culture

One of these issues that we need to face is the pace of life in modern society. The pressures to do and to achieve are extraordinary. From early life, we may have been thrust into competitive relationships with others. We learn early to evaluate ourselves in terms of our accomplishments. This can lead us into an incessant round of activities in order to remain competitive with our peers. This pace may begin to squeeze out truly restorative leisure and all sense of transcendence.

This same approach to life infiltrates ministry training programs, seminaries, and novitiates. There seems to be a lot to be accomplished before entering full-time ministry. And usually there is. But those who are responsible for programing can frustrate their very purposes by trying to accomplish too much in a limited period of time. Where programs are associated with a university calendar, for instance, the period of annual training has been reduced to eight very intense months. During two-thirds of the calendar year, the pace can become so intensive that there is little energy or time left for sustained quiet and strengthening of the spirit. The other third of the year may be spent away, usually with little faith-support from peers.

When we find ourselves living in pressure-packed situations, the crying for relief becomes very strong. We see in our culture how intensive life can easily lead to explosive release. In the present culture this seems to happen with the inappropriate use of drugs, the abuse of alcohol, and the craving for sexual release.

This also leads to violence. The shattering of nerves through the intense life and the frustrating of desires for increased gratification in this society lead to violent outbursts. Sometimes sex and violence are conjoined when both anger and lust become intertwined. Hence, the rise in violent sex crimes and the increase in sadistic or masochistic sex practices.

We need to recognize this highly-charged atmosphere and seek to work toward a climate in our own life that resists society's rhythm of life. We need to foster space and time for gentle and graceful living. There is much that we can learn from gardening. Gardeners must have deep respect for certain givens that are part of nature: namely, seed, fertile soil, moisture, sun. They can improve their quality and adjust their balance. But they cannot create the ingredients out of nothing. They receive them as gift. They cannot force growth. They learn how to prepare the soil; they sow the seed at appropriate intervals to allow enough room for the plants or vegetables; they weed in order to provide room and eliminate competition for the water and the nourishment from the soil; they try to keep a healthy balance of sun and water. But, despite the hard work involved, they know that they have to be patient, allowing time for the rhythm of growth. And the actual growth takes place quietly; almost, it seems while they are sleeping.

Perhaps, Jesus used agrarian imagery, not only because his listeners were so close to the soil, but also because there are so many helpful parallels between plant life and human growth. The sower of seed recognizes that soil which is hardened because of the footpath, or on rocky ground, or near thorny bushes will not yield long-term good fruit (Mt. 13:4-9). We, too, must be attentive to the soil in our hearts. Hearts which are too busy, too superficial, too attracted to the preoccupations of this world will fail to yield abundant fruit (Mt. 13:18-23). This is especially true when it comes to fostering a wholesome attitude toward our own bodies.

The body as sacrament

The nurturing of a holy integration of body and spirit comes hard to fallen human nature. The division within ourselves that we experience at times seem to amount to a veritable war between the body and the spirit. Actually, as Paul points out, the real struggle is between both body and soul living according to the spirit and both living according to the flesh (Gal. 5:13-26).

Just as Christ's humanity is a sacrament of his divine life, so we are truly called to allow our bodies to be sacraments of our life in Christ. True beauty and strength lies less in the natural attractiveness of the body and much more in the graced way in which the body expresses a whole person. Some of us experience tremendous self-consciousness about our bodies. We seek desperately to develop them so that they will measure up to society's standards. But beauty and strength really lie in the gentle, graceful way in which the body sacramentalizes rich inner life and a genuine caring for others. In our body, we truly worship God and serve others.

St. Paul seems to have had this in mind when he addressed the issues of sexual abuse in Corinth:

> Your body, you know, is the temple of the holy Spirit, who is in you since you received him from God. You are not your own property; you have been bought and paid for. That is why you should use your body for the glory of God.
>
> —1 Cor. 6:19-20

Paul understood that the whole person had become a new creation in Christ and that Christian sexual morality flows from this profound and liberating truth.

As psychologists who have made a study of body language can attest, a great deal of our personality is expressed in facial expression, eyes, hands, posture and gait. Part of Christian asceticism is to rediscover the ways in which the temperate satisfaction of bodily needs can support inner life and make it more possible for inner life to express itself appropriately through the body. One of the helpful insights from Zen Buddhism and Hindu Yoga is that certain bodily postures and positions support inner presence and help to express attentiveness to other individuals. A body which expresses a prayerful attitude or unfeigned welcome to others is enlivened by a strong and beautiful spirit.

Thus it is that Paul the Apostle draws his moral doctrine from his appreciation of the new creation that we are called to be in Christ Jesus. Hence, too, Paul also presents sexual immorality as prostituting Christ's body (1 Cor. 6:15), and failing to appreciate what we have become in faith (1 Cor. 6:19-20).

The Church, also, tries to find its inspiration for moral teaching in the faith realities that undergird them. Hence, the Church has tried to recognize the sacred and sacramental nature of our body, reborn in Christ and now mystically conjoined with Christ's own body.

Marital love

Some who are now being called to Church ministry, especially in the restored permanent diaconate, have also been called to marital love. For them the call to marriage has to remain more primary than any Church service. For the call to matrimony is a profound one, touching body, emotions, and spirit. It is an invitation to share in God's creative life in a very moving and engaging way. Marriage nudges the partners in a very tangible way to move beyond self-serving patterns of life in the interest of establishing and nurturing a life in common. Spouse calls spouse to better self-knowledge and more generous self-giving. Life that is shared in depth calls forth richer spiritual life. The experience of parenting invites a special share in God's creative and sustaining love. The responsibility for family allows a participation in God's providential care. Marital life is tremendously challenging and enriching.

The Church has consistently protected marital love in its teaching. This is especially evident in its insistence on the sanctity of the sexual expression of consecrated love in marriage. This warm, intimate human expression of mutual affection, acceptance and consecration includes an openness to transcendent creative mystery. Human love can so easily become self-referring, if it is not open to transcendent mystery. Whatever may be the factors which may inhibit the full realization of this sacramental act, it is intended to be the authentic expression of human marital love and to share in the mystery of divine creation. Growth toward the realization of this authentic expression depends on the gradual nurturing of this sacramental attitude toward the body and all it expresses. It is so difficult to move in this direction in a mechanized, technological age. Efficiency and pragmatic purposes so easily supercede the more deeply human and Christian values.

The same attitude of the Church is reflected in its rejection of sexual expressions which dehumanize, distort, or counterfeit the sacred marital act. The Church does not always express its teaching in the most attractive manner or with the most cogent reasoning. It is easy to point out real inadequacy in some of the use of philosophical, psychological, or theological reflections. But to reach the underlying truth that is being taught, it is important to meditate on the teaching and allow the heart and mind to be drawn to the deeper realities enshrined in it. Genital sexual love is a gift from God, good and holy. Fallen human nature experiences genital sexuality in a morally ambiguous way. Sometimes we experience our sexuality as a call to the self-transcending love of another; at other times it becomes a lustful drive for self-referring gratification. Even within marriage, there is a real asceticism to developing the capacity to let genital sexual love truly express authentic marital love in Christ. The Church's teaching points the way. It is not intended to introduce unnecesary constraints, but rather to indicate the path to wholeness and holiness. Frequently circumstances in life or emotional factors severely limit the capacity of people to approach the fullness of this teaching. This is true of our response to Church teaching in every moral area. If we can be helped to approach the Church's teaching in a meditative fashion and allow it to draw ourselves slowly beyond any limitations in our present response, then the teaching will become more life-giving for us. When we interpret moral teaching as presenting a series of extrinsic constraints, it becomes a heavy burden and the cause of depressing frustration. The lingering resentment that results can fester and block access to deeper life.

Celibate love

Many of us who are called to Church ministry have also been called to celibate life. This involves the free renunciation of genital sexual love in the faith that God's personal love is rich and more than sufficient and in the hope that the detached love of others in God's name will foster and accelerate the coming of his kingdom.

Just as many in the Church are called to image God's creative love, so some are called to image Christ's redemptive celibate love. God calls some of us to proclaim by our lives the truth that God is all. Jesus has indicated that this call is given only to some (Mt. 19:10-12). It is rooted in a deeply personal sense that God is close and drawing us into a real intimacy. This intimacy should not be exaggerated. It is not normally the exalted mystical experience of some unusually gifted people. But it is a real intimacy that involves an inner sense of God's giving of himself and of an invitation to give of self to him in return. Hence, it includes a call to spend time regularly with the loving God, to be nourished by his love and to strengthen reciprocal love. All the great world religions associate the celibate life with the gathering of inner energies, including the sexual, for greater detachment of spirit and greater union with the Divine. This is the direction in which the celibate is called.

God also calls celibates to proclaim that genital sexual experience is not necessary for genuine human love. In fact, celibacy can free us from the more exclusive marital and family love to a wider care and concern for many more people. The Christian celibate hopes to be inwardly more free to reach out to God's poor and the unloved of this world. Mother Teresa of Calcutta and her sisters give witness to the power of this kind of love in the world. But the tangible service of others is secondary to the reverential quality of that love. It is moving to notice, for instance, that a number of the homeless people touched by these Sisters of Charity in Rome appreciate the simple daily chat and prayer together more than the hot milk and sandwich. The Little Brothers and Sisters of Jesus are another remarkable witness to this. Their focus is on contemplative life during a day of hard manual work, with open hospitality to whoever comes and knocks.

Thus, the call to celibate life is a call to love. Although it does not include genital sexual experience, it is an expression of a deeper and broader sexuality which involves other-relatedness: specifically, a growing intimate relationship with God, and a genuine caring relationship with others in the concrete circumstances of life. If celibate life, therefore, becomes an excuse for selfishness, it can become a counter-sign and keep others from authentic religion.

Taking humanity seriously

We need to contemplate the idea without becoming too ethereal. We are flesh-and-blood people. If our approach becomes too spiritualized, it can seem unreal. As a result, we begin to lose the confidence in the spiritual teaching as it relates to this important area of our lives. Then we begin to counsel one another and form our own conclusions on the basis of the very confusing and often conflicting contemporary literature proffering opinions about sexual morality.

We need to appreciate that genital sexual feeling is normal and often spontaneous. It is part of being a human being. We are going to cause further trouble for ourselves, if we try to extinguish sexual drives and feelings. They will probably reemerge in a stronger and more chaotic way at a future date. The first and always the most reliable road is the humble acknowledgment of sexual feeling, drives, fantasies, and attractions in conversation with a director. Extraordinary internal pressures can seduce us into thinking that our experience of sexual desire makes us sinful, unworthy, and somehow horribly different from other people. This is especially true when highly erotic or sexually violent fantasies and desires trouble us. The most salutary advice is humble acknowledgment to a director. No other approach has more potential for diminishing the power of the drives and clarifying our understanding of what is happening.

Whether we are married or celibate, we want to move toward real, but gentle control over physical response to sexual stimuli. We do not want to try to banish feelings, drives, and physical genital responses in a harsh or rigid way. Inevitably this would lead to greater uneasiness over and preoccupation with physical purity. Rather, we seek a calm, gentle self-control which admits physical or emotional sexual feeling, but firmly directs attention to the appropriate concerns of the moment. This control leads to gentleness and reverence in marital expressions of love. Control leads the celibate to sense from within that it not only is possible, but also attractive to channel physical energies into other levels of interest and preoccupation. Both married and celibate Christians need to discover this. Usually, this process can be helped by the diminishment of other strong natural desires in the free embrace of some mortification and the quieting approach used in the beginning of our prayer. This whole process takes time. Moreover, progress can be quite uneven. Sometimes, married persons find greater inclinations to unchaste love in their middle years. Celibates may find greater sexual awareness emerging at a later time in life. Again, the approach is the same. God expects us to remain fully sexual beings with drives and affections. He offers his grace for a gradually increasing, gentle control which liberates us for deeper life.

Sexual self-stimulation can trouble us. Some enter marriage or celibate life with masturbatory habits; some experience masturbation for the first time during the period of formation; some will find their greatest struggle with it later on in life. It should be looked at honestly and seriously, but not apart from everything else that is going on in our life. Normally, it is a symptom of some other need for healing. Just as the graced integration of body and spirit manifests itself in the body becoming more and more a sacrament of divine life, so a lack of integration or an inner festering wound will eventually manifest itself in some strain experienced in the body. The medical profession testifies to this phenomenon in their diagnosis of psychosomatic illness. Masturbation can mean so many things: it may be the result of exploring our bodies out of curiosity; it may become a way of releasing tension; it may be an expression of anger at certain people or frustrating circumstances; it may be a surrender to hedonistic self-gratification; it may be a form of withdrawal from a difficult world; it may signal difficulty with intimacy; it may express desire for genital relationship.

We do not want to rivet attention on the masturbatory behavior. Rather, we want to seek help in achieving some humble understanding of its meaning in our life. Our fantasy may be an important clue, especially the fantasy that accompanies the act itself. Because this can be embarrassing and humiliating for us, we can find ourselves hesitant to share these fantasies. But in bringing them into the open with a sensitive and competent director, we can be helped to see the very normal dimensions to our inner life. Although each of us is unique, the general patterns are common. Our attention should not be directed to the images of the fantasy, but to the inner feelings and experience that accompany the fantasy. We must be very cautious here. We can deal safely in spiritual direction only with the meaning that easily becomes conscious. If the meaning is unconscious, it is more appropriate to work with a good psychologist or psychiatrist.

Recognition of the meaning of masturbatory behavior is only part of the process. Eventually we want to become more free of this kind of enslavement. We will want to treat the inner wound and to develop approaches to life that handle the inner difficulty or tension better. We will want to continue to acknowledge this struggle from time to time without making it the primary topic of conversation with our director. A good director will assist us to appreciate the body as a sacrament of the whole person, to expand our own heart in concern for others, and to embrace those ascetical practices which seem most appropriate to our inner needs. We will come to recognize the special healing grace of the sacraments, especially the sacrament of reconciliation. Above all, we need to grow in the humility which recognizes that God is the primary healer, the patience which permits ourselves a slow and gradual journey and the gift of compassion in understanding the weakness of others as a result of our own experience.

One of the realities that our sexuality points to is the need for human relationship. We cannot even be born without relationship. Moreover, healthy family relationship supports wholesome maturation as we grow up. Adults also need good peer relationships. Hopefully, the married find this in an especially saving way in their relationship with their spouses. Celibates also need wholesome friendship. Good peer friendship is maturing and freeing. It keeps alive a special kind of caring for others. It helps to make us more honest and accountable. It also brings some measure of human support and understanding. In Church ministry, it can also be a special encouragement for inner life, if there is some mutual sharing in the life of faith. Peer friendship for adults more often is with those of one's own sex. But it is also true that man-woman, non-marital friendships can be quite salutary.

What, then, is the reason why spiritual formation in the recent past has generally discouraged friendship? As always, a gift of God can be misused. And over-zealous directors sometimes preferred strict abstinence to running the risk of abuse.

There are some signals to be alert to in these friendships. The first is exclusivity. An increasingly exclusive preoccupation with each other usually means an immature fascination with the other person, accompanied by enslaving demands placed on each other. This kind of relationship eventually becomes suffocating and usually ends abruptly when one or the other can handle it no longer. A second signal is a growing sexual preoccupation. Emotional and physical drives become too prominent. A person cannot spend much time alone. There is a pressing need to do everything together. There is a resulting jealousy of any freedom that the other enjoys in human relationships and activities. There is little capacity for prayerful solitude. Lastly, there sometimes is a diminishing respect for the integrity of self and the other. Instead, there is almost a compulsive need to reveal oneself unconditionally and a desire to psychologically rape the other. Obviously, these signals spell trouble and mean that human friendship has gone astray. Such developments can bring a great deal of pain to those involved. Usually, simple, direct honesty with a spiritual director is the greatest safeguard against such tragedy.

On the other hand, good peer friendships are rooted in two people being utterly clear about their own identities and commitments. There is a real respect and reverence for each other. There is a sincere desire to support the experience of God and greater sacrificial love for others, even if neither surfaces that explicitly in ordinary conversation. In fact, more often than not, the deeper things are more presumed and silently provide the basis for strong, supportive friendship.

Overt sexual activity, or the kind of tactile affection which normally induces genital expressions of love, of course, undercut genuine Christian friendship. Whether it be heterosexual or homosexual, it immediately rushes two people into an emotional and physical vise. Their lives suddenly become tremendously entangled. If it has happened by accident, then it is important to acknowledge it, repent, seek healing and find the necessary distance in the relationship. A compassionate and firm spiritual director can provide great healing by neither condemning nor condoning (Jn. 8:11). We need to address the whole situation and find the grace of humble self-knowledge, the experience of deeper inner conversion, and the strength to restructure our approaches to life in a more salutary way. If the overt sexual activity is repeated and deliberate, then we need to accept reality. This behavior is utterly incompatible with the consecrated love of marriage or celibacy. We need to reassess the appropriateness of our desire for public Church ministry.

Individuals moving into ecclesial ministry want to have a good ability to live and work harmoniously with others before embracing a Church life on a premanent basis. Married persons need to respect the call to celibate love. Celibates need to reverence the call to marriage. Men and women need to be able to collaborate with one another with great respect for the complementary gifts each brings. The last thing that the Church needs today is a sex war in trying to determine appropriate collaboration between men and women in public Church life and mission. It also involves reasonably good relationships with persons in positions of authority. The Church needs neither sycophants nor rebels for the fruitful pursuit of its redemptive mission. In sum, the Church wants men and women who are capable of genuine oblative love in their dedication to God and God's people.

Counter-signs to chaste love

Chaste love is a grace. It is an important condition for Church ministry since public representatives of Christ reveal more about God's love for his people through the integrity of their own love than by their teaching or pastoral care. So, it is important to limit access to this public call only to those who have a reasonable hope of being able to live a chaste love.

If, then, we handle genital impulses only with great discomfort after attempting to face this over a period of time with help, we are probably going to find public Church ministry a great strain. We may find ourselves entrapped in obsessive masturbatory activity and on-going preoccupation with genital gratification. We may find ourselves overly conscious of sexual feeling and desire in relationship with others. We may begin to act out our sexual desires heterosexually or homosexually.

In all of these cases, whether married or celibate, we have not found a sufficiently calm, gentle control which then frees up inner energies and attention for deeper spiritual life and a greater capacity to help others discover the grace of chaste love.

Secondly, if we seek Church ministry after having entered an unhappy marriage or find ourselves accepting the commitment to celibacy only because it is a necessary condition for the kind of ministry we desire, we are sowing the seeds of serious difficulty for ourselves later on. If we have not discovered the inner richness of marital life or the inner attractiveness of celibate life, we will run the risk of becoming unloving and unloveable persons. Some inner appreciation of our sexual consecration is a necessary condition for growth in the life. We can hardly avoid inner resistance and resentment, if we are basically unhappy about our sexual consecration.

This second difficulty is expressed more often in act than in words if we cannot or will not renounce exclusive, intimate relationships which run the risk of undermining our more primary commitment. If we are married, we may be acting out some serious dissatisfaction in our marriage. If we are celibate, we may be expressing the need or desire for closer life-long companionship than celibate life can provide. In either case, it is more honest and forthright to face what this really means for our future before blindly plunging into a life of escalating inner conflict.

There is another context in which the way we act may reveal more than our words. As potential Church ministers, we can use our status to play with the emotional response of others. We may have little direct consciousness of what we are doing. But male candidates for Church ministry, for example, may enter the lives of young women and manifest great personal concern and affection which touches them deeply and arouses the feeling that they care in a very special way. The women "fall in love." But the men have little or no intention of pursuing the relationship any further. They have proven to themselves that they are capable of winning the affections of a young woman. The women, meanwhile, are devastated and left emotionally hurt and angry. Women candidates, although with more difficulty, can do the same with men.

In all these cases, we may need the helping role of others to interpret our behavior and postpone further consideration of Church ministry until such tendencies can be adequately faced. We may find this conclusion difficult to accept if there are excessive needs operative in our lives. But it is important to be realistic and face these serious discrepancies rather than permit the inevitable unhappiness for ourselves as well as for those whose lives we touch.

Marriage is more than a secular union between two people. It is a sacrament that symbolizes Christ's spousal union with his Church and offers to men and women a real share in God's creative love. Only those married persons who have touched the real grace of marital life and love ought to enter public Church ministry.

Celibacy is a gift, a grace, a mystery. It is a way of loving that calls into question some generally accepted convictions in the present culture; namely, the need for genital sexual expression of love; the fear that solitude is the cause of loneliness; the inclination to define masculinity or femininity in terms of physical sexual attractiveness; the cult of self-fulfillment and self-gratification. Because celibate love is a mysterious reality, it calls for a great deal of faith, a great amount of prayer, and a great desire for spiritual depth. In the priesthood and religious life, it has a special power of proclaiming that God's love is sufficient in life. Only those celibates who touch the inner grace of celibate life and love ought to consider moving into public Church ministry.

SEEKING DETACHMENT IN LIFE

Just as chaste love touches the way we enter into relationship with God and other people, so detachment from riches affects the way we approach the possession and accumulation of things in this world. There is a close link between the quality of our response to the call to chaste love and the generosity of our response to the call to be poor. Charles Davis once drew attention to this truth for all who consecrate themselves to celibate love. Just a few months before he announced his intention to leave the celibate priesthood and to marry, he wrote:

> The chief problem with celibacy today is that its meaning is obscured almost beyond recognition without poverty. An eschatological sign is unconvincing when its bearer is securely ensconced in material comfort, whether personal or communal. The accent then shifts to the negation of sex, and the celibate himself loses sight of the personal nature of the values he has renounced and wrongly finds compensation in material things. This is detrimental to his own personality, because it blunts his perception of the right order of things. And it spoils his witness. A comfortable bachelordom is no sign of the Kingdom. So people, including disillusioned celibates, look to marriage to rediscover the personal element in the Christian message.[1]

These words express both the great challenge and the great risk of celibate love in Church ministry. The celibate *should* become freer for more detachment in life.

The call to become poor for Christ is, in an analagous way, *an invitation* given to the married disciple as well. Unfortunately, witness to simplicity of life seems rare in our western world. In fact, it seems to be left to the more heroic to embrace this detachment in concrete life. Certainly, one of the authentic signs of sanctity is the practice of using the goods of this world only insofar as they give glory to God and offer redemptive service to others and abstaining from them whenever they become an obstacle or a snare.[2]

Perhaps the Church in the free western world will be judged in history for its approach to this issue during the twentieth century. We are called especially in this age, to recognize the demands of justice and the need for a better distribution of this world's goods. Underlying it all, our belief in transcendent mystery is at stake. Do we really believe that God

[1]Charles Davis, "Theological Asides," *America,* Vol. 114 (1966), p. 420.

[2]Ignatius of Loyola, *The Spiritual Exercises,* "The Principle and Foundation."

has created all the things of this world as expressions of his love? Do we truly believe that God personally cares for us no matter how much we have or do not have? Do we believe that God is the common father of all people and that we are called to live in a world family? Do we receive the goods we have with grateful hearts and want to share them with others? Do we have the courage to renounce in faith some of our possessions for God's sake and the sake of fellow human beings in need?

The call to be poor

In order to appreciate better what may be involved in God's call to be poor, let us look first at the Scriptures. Poverty has more than one meaning in the Old Testament. The patriarchs interpreted wealth as a sign of God's blessing and poverty as a curse; but the prophets decried those who avariciously took advantage of those who were defenseless and deprived them of what was rightly theirs or those who arrogantly placed all their security in their riches in this world; finally, the wisdom authors wrestled with the ambiguous meaning of poverty and concluded that God's chosen ones were the *anawim:* that is, those who in the midst of suffering, oppression, or want placed their hope and confidence in Yahweh.

The New Testament makes it clear that the disciple is to adopt the mind and heart of Christ Jesus: "His state was divine, yet he did not cling to his equality with God but emptied himself to assume the condition of a slave, and became as men are; and being as men are, he was humbler yet, even to accepting death, death on a cross" (Phil. 2:6-8). The gospel accounts are replete with details about the way in which Christ lived out this self-emptying from birth in a cave to death on the cross.

In addition to the remarkable testimony of his life, Jesus also made it clear in his teaching that the blessed are the poor in spirit (Mt. 5:3); his disciples were not to store up treasures on earth lest they ensnare the heart (Mt. 6:19-21); nor were they to try to serve both God and money (Mt. 6:24); rather, they were to trust more in God's providential care and let their primary concern be for his kingdom (Mt. 25-34). Probably the strongest statement Jesus made to the rich and powerful was expressed in the story of the rich man and Lazarus (Lk. 16:19-31). The gospel passage that most unsettles the would-be disciple is the invitation which Jesus eventually gave to the rich young man who wanted eternal life: "Jesus looked steadily at him and loved him, and he said, 'There is one thing you lack. Go, and sell everything you own and give the money to the poor, and you will have treasure in heaven; then, come, follow me' " (Mk. 10:21-22).

Like the gospel call to chaste love, Christ's call to become poor calls first for prayerful meditation. The radical expression of this call reveals how deeply rooted is the need for conversion in this area. The gospel is not calling merely for a reshuffling of a few priorities. Jesus is asking for purity or undividedness of heart (Mt. 5:1). He is asking that we love God with our whole heart (Lk. 10:27). In this sense, there can be no compromise, even though we never fully realize this total dedication. Ultimately, we want to be grasped completely and definitively by the Lord. In effect, this never happens perfectly until we literally give up everything we have in this world at our death and join the Lord forever in the next.

What, then, does this call to be poor mean in practice?

Destitution

Sometimes it is easier to respond to such a challenging question by stating what that call does *not* mean. Christ did not intend that his disciples become destitute or that his Church condone destitution. Michael Harrington's *Other America* and Barbara Ward's *The Rich Nations and the Poor Nations,* appearing in print during the same year, documented the extraordinary social and economic inequities, both in the United States and throughout the world. For many Americans, it was the first time that the harsh realities of some pockets of destitution invaded their consciousness. Within a few short years, activists of all ages mobilized forces that led to a Peace Corps, a Job Corps, an anti-Poverty Program, increased foreign aid and an ambitious plan for the Great Society. Lay people, priests, and religious assumed some leadership roles in these campaigns to fight poverty. Paradoxically, fifteen years after the start of this concerted effort, the gap between the rich and the poor seems disappointingly greater and in a period of a strained world economy, the voices calling for retrenchment in spending for services to the poor are carrying more weight everywhere.

But destitution is a real evil. This can be verified in places close to home. It is especially evident in some Third World situations. There can be no disputing the Christian intuition that Christ's call to become poor cannot be construed as a defense for destitution. Nor does Jesus' prophetic comment that the world will always have its poor (Mt. 26:11) justify apathy in the face of such blatant injustice. The poverty of Christ is not destitution. Rather, we are called to alleviate it with all the courage, imagination, and power we can devise.

One Christian response: common ownership

We have always realized that Christ's call to be poor includes both personal renunciation and some effective concern for the poor. Some Christians from the very beginning were inspired to own everything in common (Acts 2:44). "The whole group of believers was united, heart and soul; no one claimed for his own use anything that he had, as everything they owned was held in common (Acts. 4:32). Although this approach never worked out perfectly, even from the beginning (Acts 5:1-11), nevertheless, religious communities in the Church have sensed a value to this approach and have consistently tried to embrace this form of poverty over the centuries. The surrender of the right to private ownership has the advantage of responding literally to the invitation given to the young rich man. There is an absolute "selling" or divesting oneself of all that a person owns *personally* for the sake of a common ownership in following Christ.

There is a special wisdom in this approach. The surrender of the right to personal ownership is radical. It cuts deeply into the human heart. It calls us to that single-heartedness which is central to genuine discplieship. It leads us into the experience of dependence on others who exercise a certain control over us even in the basic necessities of life. It means that we suffer the same fortunes, good or ill, that the whole community experiences. This can be freeing even as it is risky. Each of us is expected to contribute according to means; each is expected to receive according to need.

Mismanagement, authoritarianism, lack of personal responsibility and community selfishness are all part of the real risk. Instead of radical discipleship, the community as a whole can become just as entrenched in attachment to the comforts of this world. Those in administrative roles may see themselves more as managers of a large portfolio; members of the community may become quite dependent and demanding people. Every generation in a community needs, in a sense, to rediscover the original meaning of common ownership: detachment from the ordinary human craving to possess things for self; the pooling of resources so that members in need may not go wanting; the sharing of any surplus with the poor outside the community.

It is a hopeful sign to see efforts being made, even in capitalistic economies, to introduce some of the inspiration for Christian common ownership into agriculture, business, and government. Many attempts have been made on the part of volunteers, local organizers or religious groups to foster cooperatives for poorer people in food, clothing, and money. Capitalistic governments have introduced some important social reforms which allow the government to collect high taxes from those who have more and offer needed services for the poor.

In one of the most provocative books to emerge recently in the field of economics, *Small is Beautiful,* the late Ernst Schumacher called into question some generally assumed principles in economics. He proposed as a desirable and viable alternative the approach of the Scott Bader Company in England. This company was originally founded in 1920. In 1951, the owner transferred ownership to all who worked in the company and established a constitution with all the workers. It was not just an experiment in profit-sharing. It constituted common ownership. This constitution regulated size of the company, remuneration for work, processes for hiring and dismissal, appointment of the Board of Directors and the allocation of profits, including money for taxes, refinancing and charitable ventures. Despite dire predictions, the company has increased its sales eight times over and quadrupled its net profits. This respected British economist proposed common ownership without the complexities of socialist government ownership or the extremes of marxist governmental control; favored limitation in size to avoid the disproportionate power of multinational corporations and to provide for personal participation on the part of all workers; promoted strong social consciousness to improve certain dehumanizing social conditions and to forge a more responsible collaboration between business and the concerns of government.

On the domestic scene, it may also be enlightening to note that family life has traditionally respected the principle of common ownership. It is true that in recent years, married couples and even children have begun to maintain separate titles of ownership to property and other resources. But ordinarily, family life has known the experience of common ownership under one name. This is a way in which married disciples can truly overcome possessiveness and share God's gifts with one another and their families.

Common ownership has, then, been one of the principal ways that Christian disciples have sought to follow Christ's call to be poor. It offers real possibilities for deeper inner freedom. It can also be subverted into selfishness. But it is a path some Christians have explored.

New dimensions to the response:
the struggle for social justice

We have always realized that the Christian call to renounce some goods in this world for the sake of the kingdom is intended to make effective concern for the poor more possible. The experience of our present century has impressed on us how much the plight of the poor seems to be inextricably linked with our economic, social, and political systems. In a sense, Karl Marx was a prophet when he perceived this in the early decades following the rise of industrialism in the west. The papal social encyclicals of the past ninety years, the pastoral constitution on the Church in the modern world (*Gaudium et spes*), the 1971 statement of the International Synod of Bishops, all draw our attention to the world's search for a Christian social order and the mission of the Church in contributing to this struggle. We cannot any longer see the concern for the poor in solely individual terms. The evils that the poor face are systemic.

In the wake of the first Conference of Latin American bishops in Medellin, Colombia in 1968, there has emerged a new and challenging approach to spirituality. This liberation Christianity has captured the imagination of many who witness the powerlessness and hopelessness of oppressed peoples. The liberation writers take very seriously the peculiar economic, political, and social situation in Latin America. They turn to the Scriptures and find there that it was the exodus event which really prepared the Jewish people for God. They had been an oppressed, disillusioned and fragmented people until God led them under the guidance of Moses into resistance, rebellion and release. This saving event for the people of old led them to faith and covenant. This experience is then seen as a paradigm for the way God wants to continue to enter human history to save his people.

The liberationists rightly draw attention to the social dimensions to redemption. Both original sin and personal sin influence the very social structures of our lives. The conditions of severe deprivation, perpetuated by the systematic violence of oppressive social policies and practices, constitute an injustice that cries to heaven for vengeance. Salvation from sin, then, has profoundly social implications and involves liberation from desperate living conditions. It is impossible to restrict the redemptive experience to a merely individualistic salvation.

We can learn much from these insights, even if we recognize the need to eschew an exclusively Marxist interpretation of the social struggle or the use of violence in trying to promote greater justice. There is no single Christian way to approach this challenge of social justice. Each of us is called according to our own specific gifts and vocation. Obviously, any direct involvement in this arena of social change demands a rigorous asceticism of a Church leader. Credibility among the dispossessed is earned only by authenticity in personal life. And daily involvement in the struggle of the poor is extremely draining. Only a lively faith in the transcendent salvation God wants to effect for his people can help such leaders to sustain inner life and enter into long-term service. It is so important for Church leaders to keep their mission clearly in view. The Church does not promise a social salvation. The Church concerns itself with social justice because economic, social, and political conditions are real human factors which either tend to support or undermine a life open to faith and transcendent salvation. God ordinarily asks us to do our best to foster social conditions which support Christian life in our world.

Personalizing the response

In responding to both the call to be poor in Christ and to be concerned for Christ's poor, there are some concrete ways in which those of us who may not be called to direct social action may still take seriously

Christ's invitation. First, we want to beg God's grace for a less divided heart. This is the central issue. There are so many competing gods that creep into the lives of even the most sincere. The desire for success, achievement, honors, recognition, acclaim and gratification can subtly take over. They become idols that are worshipped. The attempt to attain these can consume a great deal of attention and energy. In Matthew's gospel account, there is a close relationship between the first and sixth beatitudes which Jesus uttered: "How happy are the poor in spirit" (Mt. 5:3), and "Happy the pure in heart" (Mt. 5:8). Both point to the value of an undivided heart: the first emphasizes detachment from anything that stands in the way of God; the second encourages the nurturing of the one and only desire which is absolutely necessary, the desire for God. To encourage poverty without focusing on this inner spirit would distort the meaning of Christ's call to be poor.

Then, as we become engaged in Church ministry, we can begin to put flesh and blood on this inner spirit. The detached love of God ought to free us for more concerned love for God's friends. For instance, in ministry-training programs, we want to learn to put the authentic needs of others above our own personal whims. There is a real poverty involved in developing a *reasonable* availability to people. Also, as we look forward to more formal ministry in the future, we will want to move beyond the inclination to limit our focus to certain kinds of parishes or living situations or areas of work. This is always a great temptation, especially as we are being given more of a role today in the ultimate determination of a pastoral assignment.

Moreover, it is good to be attentive to our own reaction to work which bears little or no visible fruit. Apparent failure can be discouraging to us, especially if we see others working more successfully. If we can learn to labor quietly and perseveringly without much tangible fruit, we are learning a great deal about poverty in action.

Sometimes, the opportunities of being poor in the gospel sense are so close to us that we miss them. For example, there is an art to living simply in clothes, tastes, and decoration. It has to do with an attitude which receives what is available with gratitude and without grumbling, and then works with it creatively. There is a great difference between expensive clothes and simple, tasteful ones which express our inner self. Rich food is for the wealthy; substantial, nourishing food for the easily satisfied. It is one thing to decorate in a cluttered or gaudy fashion; it is quite another to accent simple natural beauty.

We live in an age of excessive consumerism. Business creates markets by persuading us that we have more needs and desires than we initially recognized: expensive foods and drink, luxurious hi-fi's and computer-regulated television sets, radio-alarm clocks and electric tooth brushes, CB radios and tape decks. The list is interminable. Can we begin to resist the seductions of this world?

Married persons may want to search out a moderate style of life which rightly meets the legitimate needs of a family in an economically complex society. The higher the standard of life we accustom ourselves to, the more we will be inclined to look for ways to support it, even at the expense of possibilities in Church ministry. It should always be recognized, however, that if the demands of ministry place an exaggerated strain on the family, it is more important to be faithful to the marital and familial concerns. Thus, a desire to live in the inner city, among the dispossessed or in the Third World may have to yield to family realities. God wants us to serve in accordance with our gifts and responsibilities in life.

Celibates should experience more freedom to be poor because they ordinarily do not have the responsibility of caring financially for others. It is so important to shun the comfortable, self-centered life. As Charles Davis perceptively suggested in the quotation found at the beginning of this chapter, comfortable bachelordom besmirches the sign of true celibate witness. It actually suggests a settling in to the good life in *this* world. We want to resist this tendency within ourselves. It is, therefore, important to adopt a simple and unpretentious level of life. We want to do an honest day's work without grumbling and complaining—or, on the other hand, without becoming workaholics. Recreation can be modest and simple. It is so helpful to discover ways to enter into truly restorative and refreshing leisure while shunning that kind of recreation which is more dissipative of the human spirit or beyond the financial possibilities of the ordinary person. Ordinarily, it is good for us to be firm in refusing "privilege" lest we begin to move into a stratum of society that is restricted to a few and lest we begin to become a parasite and a pawn of the rich.

This is especially true for the diocesan seminarian. One day he hopes to belong to a real fraternity with his fellow diocesan priests and his bishop. This fraternity has true sacramental bonds which unite members of the ordained priesthood with one another and with the visible head of Christ's body. However real the sacramental bonds are, they do not forge the kind of juridical community which calls for the surrender of private ownership, the sharing of goods and the pledge of mutual support in time of need. Although this commitment to one another does not formally exist by virtue of a vowed life, the diocese does assume a certain basic responsibility to offer a minimum salary and board and room. Most dioceses have established a common fund to finance reasonable medical expenses and a modest retirement. Moreover, most diocesan priests find the ordinary people quite generous in supplementary ways. So, the diocesan seminarian in America can ordinarily expect to find himself in the priesthood with sufficient financial support. It behooves him, therefore, not to lay up treasures in this world and not to lose a real concern for the poor.

Our approach to the call to poverty is not fully adequate without some tangible service to the poor. We are asked to be stewards of our own resources. They are ultimately gifts given by God in trust. No matter how minimal this may have to be at times, we should set aside some limited money, saved through self-denial, for the poor. The fostering of this approach to life keeps alive a consciousness of those who are much more in need. If the gift to the needy can be done personally, this has certain advantages. If it is done through an organization, we may want to give preference to those organizations which try to break the cycle of poverty or promote the redemptive mission of Christ among the poor.

Moreover, it seems good to become acquainted with some individual poor people through visiting or other forms of ministry. If we cultivate a sensitivity for the poor, we will want to serve among the poor either among those less well off in ordinary parishes or in those areas which are severely deprived.

Without becoming an ideologue for any particular issue, we will want to keep Christ's mission to the poor alive in the hearts of our fellow Christians. Good preaching and teaching in this area will flow from our reading, pondering, and contemplative concern for those in need and least able to help themselves.

Christ's call to become poor, then, is a call to simplicity of life. It involves a growing purity of heart and the developing art of letting one's inner contemplative love of the Lord shine forth in a graceful and simple approach to personal life as well as in a genuine love of God's poor. This poverty of spirit opens the heart for obedience to God's word wherever it may be spoken.

DISCOVERING THE MYSTERY OF OBEDIENCE

The post-World War II generation has very ambivalent feelings about obedience. The issues which were raised in the Nuremburg trials haunt the memories of many people. For the first time, an international court of justice established that there are certain universal human rights and values which no national or local authority can arbitrarily deny or force others to deny. The proffered defense of obedience to commands which called for the systematic extermination of the Jewish people did not exonerate the individuals of their personal culpability in perpetrating horrible mass murders. These trials represented a dramatic breakthrough in international law and justice. Their impact has been reverberating ever since.

Although the principle of civil disobedience has a long and hallowed standing in the Judaeo-Christian tradition, it has been more and more recognized universally in the decades since the war. Mahatma Gandhi appealed to it in South Africa to win equal justice for his Indian people and then in India to secure independence from England. Martin Luther King, Jr. became a national and international symbol of the black struggle for equality by his invoking of this principle and his use of Gandhi's techniques of non-violent resistance. Some of the liberationists in Third-World countries have been inspired by the principles of civil disobedience. The anti-war movement in the United States employed many forms of peaceful resistance to influence the eventual pull-out of American troops from Vietnam.

It is no wonder that the present generation has grown up with a real suspicion of authority and institution. While there are many who seek to restore the unquestioning loyalty and obedience which more frequently marked the past, post-Nixonian America is generally quite cautious about blind obedience. Why, then, does the Church insist on obedience in the Church minister?

The obedience Christ taught

From the beginning of his earthly life, the Son of God was obedient. He embraced the will of his Father (Hb. 10:5-7). It was a perduring characteristic of Jesus' spirituality that he continually found his nourishment in doing the Father's will (Jn. 4:34). This desire to seek out and fulfill the Father's plan was especially manifest in his passion (Mt. 26:36-46). On the cross, Jesus expressed his readiness to hand himself entirely over to his Father (Lk. 23:46) and then proclaimed his work to be finished (Jn. 19:30). Paul would later understand that the reason the

Father raised Jesus and exalted him above all was that he had humbled himself to become man and in obedience had accepted the ignominious death on a cross (Phil. 2:6-8).

His approach to life Jesus also enjoined on his disciples. He taught his disciples to pray: "Your will be done on earth as it is in heaven" (Mt. 6:10). And he stated that authentic relationship with him depended on doing the will of his Father in heaven (Mt. 12:50).

Obedience to God also involves obedience to human authority, civil and religious. Jesus indicated to Pilate that Pilate's authority was a share in divine authority (Jn. 19:11). He had previously taught, in response to the dilemma posed by the Pharisees about tribute to Caesar that civil authority could make legitimate demands as long as it did not violate the place of God in human life (Mt. 22:15-22). Paul insisted that every Christian was obligated to cooperate with civil authority, "since all government comes from God" and "anyone who resists authority is rebelling against God's decision" (Rm. 13:1-2). Peter also made it clear that Christ's disciples were not only to obey God, but all subordinate officials, such as the emperor and governors for the sake of God (1 Pt. 2:13-15). Slaves, in the social climate of Paul's time, were to obey their masters (Eph. 6:5); women, in accordance with the familial structure of the time, were to be subject to the authority of their husbands (1 Cor. 11:3); children were to accept the authority of their parents (Col. 3:20).

This requirement of obedience on the part of subjects, included also certain expectations for rulers. They were ever to be conscious of the origin of their authority and the consequent implication of their accountability before God (Jn. 19:11). In the Christian community, there was no place for authoritarianism. Leaders were to consider themselves the servants of all (Mk.10:43-45). Shepherds of the flock of God were to watch over, "not simply as a duty but gladly, because God wants it; not for sordid money, but because you are eager to do it. Never be a dictator over any group that is put in your charge, but be an example that the whole flock can follow" (1 Pt. 5:2-3). The same Paul who expected obedience from slaves toward their masters, urged Philemon to accept back his run-away slave, not as a slave but as a "dear brother" (Philemon 16); the Paul who asked the woman to recognize the headship of her husband, enjoined husbands to "love their wives just as Christ loved the Church and sacrificed himself for her" (Eph. 5:25); the Paul who reminded children of their duty to obey their parents, asked parents never to drive their "children to resentment but in bringing them up correct them and guide them as the Lord does" (Eph. 6:4).

Toward an understanding of obedience

Christian obedience, therefore, cannot be reduced to a merely juridical reality. It touches the whole relationship which we experience with God and human, civil, or religious leaders. It is intimately related to faith.

In faith, we recognize that our life is a gift from God. Hence, we wish to listen (*ob-audire*) to the heart of God who brought us into being in order that we might discover our own purpose and destiny. This listening to God with the intention of doing what is heard is the root of obedience. God's inner designs are partially hidden in mystery. They are also manifest in concrete ways in the life, death, and resurrection of his Son; in the teaching he entrusted to his Church, partly in the inspired Scripture and partly in the authentic interpretation offered by the college of bishops in union with the bishop of Rome; in the laws of legitimate government in human society; in the domestic relationships of family; in the authorities of freely chosen religious communities; in the concrete circumstances of life over which a person has little or no control.

This willingness to listen deeply with the intention of doing what God wants as manifest in these ways is at the heart of obedience. It involves a communion with the heart of Jesus. It is not focused so much on the concrete norm or expectation, but on the inner readiness of spirit to respond. Besides being grounded in faith, it is an expression of hope that God will triumph even if we do not fully appreciate the value of what we are being asked to do. If we are humble, we will recognize the real limitations of our own human knowledge and perspective. We will have learned from the past some of the prejudices or myopia that control our minds. We will want, then, to be open to being drawn beyond our present horizons.

Obedience, of course, also chastens the human will. Resistance to authority is deep within us. Even those of us who have come from homes where authority was exercised well, can experience considerable difficulty. Inevitably, we seek to move toward a healthy independence from parental direction. Yet, as we move into Church ministry, the emphasis on obedience to other authorities or the free embrace of the authority of a religious institution can, at first, seem to sabotage the movement toward a rightful autonomy. But, once this transition is made in a healthy, successful way, then we recognize that the greatest enemies to Christian maturity really lie *within*. We find, for instance, that our own undisciplined impulses and strong wilfulness are the stronger obstacles to discovering and living the happiness God wills. That is one reason why mature obedience purifies the will.

No virtue remains Christian if it is separated from charity. It is charity that both provides the inspiration and the safeguards for authentically Christian obedience. The human family and the ecclesial family need some concrete structures to express unity and resist harmful disintegration. Authority, then, becomes the sacrament of God's presence with a very significant role to nurture and strengthen a rightful unity. The or-

A Practical Guide To Spiritual Formation

dinary disciple, out of love for others, wants to collaborate with that authority to foster the same unity and resist the forces of unnecessary division.

The ambivalence that law arouses

There is no doubt that society needs civil law and that religious society needs church law. Civil law grows out of a political system and tries to express or safeguard a responsible balance between the exercise of inviolable human rights and the minimal constraints necessary for common government to promote order, justice, and peace. Church law grows out of a religious organization which tries to express or present revealed truth as it applies to the normal living situations. In both cases, unless a person has been personally involved in the formulation of the specific laws, the law can be experienced as extrinsic to the person. It comes from others. It seems to be a means of constraint and it arouses ambivalent feelings in the ordinary person. Law is necessary; yet, law is also resented.

Paul recognized the ambivalence aroused in us by moral law. Although Paul can hardly be called antinomian, he made it clear that moral law often even occasions sin because the forbidding of a particular gratification to fallen human nature sometimes increases its fascinating attraction (Rm. 7:7). It seems to be merely an external norm which confines and limits attractive desires, thereby increasing their allure. Sometimes it makes holiness of life that much harder.

That is why Paul proclaimed that we are free of this kind of constraining law (Rm. 7:6). For, if we are truly living our baptismal incorporation in Christ Jesus, we are more and more impelled from within to live the life-giving truths enshrined in the law (Rm. 7:4-6). We will have laid hold of an inner law of the spirit which sets us free from the negative influence of a law that seems to be merely an external constraint (Rm. 8:1). This inner law of the spirit frees us, not for licentiousness, but for the living of a truly spiritual life; that is, a life dominated by God's Spirit (Rm. 8:5-17). It draws us beyond the issue of slavish compliance to laws and moves us to seek inwardly a more generous response to God's plan (Rm. 7:14-15).

What, then, is the role of law for us Christians? It is a real, although admittedly limited good. The civil law of legitimate government is normally an expression of God's desire to allow secular governments to share in his authority and guide human society toward a just and peaceful order. Religious law enshrines life-giving truth. To the extent that we have not yet experienced inner conversion of heart and touched the inner law of the Spirit, it points the way to true liberty. It is educative and binding. If we have entered into an adult conversion and discovered the inner dynamic of the Spirit prompting us to make responses that go far beyond the law, we are freed from the troublesome constraints of the law. We need experience them only when we misuse our freedom for licentiousness and once again need to be reminded of the truth by the medicinal constraints of the law.

Lawrence Kohlberg[1] charts the various stages which mark progress in the development of a more mature conscience. The earlier stages depend on punishment and reward as motives for moral compliance; later, peer values or pressures and enforced laws in society supply the motivating force; ideally the person eventually moves to moral decision based an inner perception of value. This theory regarding the maturation of conscience can help to interpret both the different ways in which we experience moral life along life's journey and the differing approaches taken by other people in this age of pluralism in moral questions. One factor, however, deserves special attention. For the Christian, the law as motivating factor belongs not just to one stage of moral development. Law has a special pedagogical role in the early period of moral development insofar as it points the way to a reliable road to freedom. Law also has a pedagogical role in the later stages insofar as *meditation* on the law is the vehicle for deepening insight and eventually embracing the life-giving truths contained within the law. The law in the early periods is experienced as binding and constraining; it arouses resentment and fascination with the forbidden fruit. The law in the later periods of development is experienced as binding, yet freeing; it leads to a far deeper love for and doing of the truth.

Conditions for a Christian obedience to law

Even while treating the evangelical approach to law, we want to realize that there are certain real conditions for *Christian* obedience to any law. Some of these conditions relate to the authority that introduces and enforces the law or the content of the laws themselves; some relate to the way in which Christians collaborate with persons in authority and obey their commands.

For a law to command moral compliance, it must first of all be instituted by a legitimate authority acting within the bounds of that authority. For instance, an illegally-elected public official or a schismatic bishop cannot issue laws or commands that bind in conscience. Moreover, if the law or command is contrary to God's law, it is not binding. Thus, Peter and the apostles were able to say to the high priest and the Sanhedrin: "Obedience to God comes before obedience to men" (Acts 5:28). In imitation of them, and on the same grounds, countless martyrs have refused to offer worship to human

[1]Cf. Kohlberg & Turel, eds., *Moralization Research, The Cognitive Development Approach* (N.Y.: Holt, Rinehart & Winston, 1971).

rulers or to comply with other laws which required apostasy or immoral conduct. Authentically Christian civil disobedience rests on these principles. We refuse to surrender our credal or moral responsibilities. But we freely accept the consequences of our technical violation of the law. This takes real moral courage and inner strength, particularly when the issues are sometimes blurred in the human situation.

Beyond these crucially important considerations, the *approach* that we, as Christians, take to obedience demands some reflection. We are not to be passive. We have a call to participate actively and responsibly in decision-making in society, in Church, and especially in areas that particularly touch our own life. We help persons in authority to make more enlightened decisions by supplying helpful data that they may not have readily at their disposal. If the deliberations have a particular significance for our own personal life, we may want to offer personal data and even indicate our preferences if good reasons support them. Ultimately, then, responsible participation in the process also includes a readiness to accept the ultimate decision rendered by legitimate authority. If this decision subsequently occasions serious hardship, we can request a review of the decision, report on our further experience and again indicate our desire to find God's plan in whatever new decision is reached. This kind of participation according to our role should be encouraged by the very style of training we enter. Active participation in decision-making avoids a passive dependency and encourages mature, responsible obedience.

Obedience facilitates heroism

Have you ever wondered what enables a person to move beyond the ordinary to the heroic? Obviously, outstanding sacrificial charity is central. But perhaps the particular aspect of charity which is involved is that inner largeness of heart which senses a call to fulfill a law beyond the ordinary. What motivated Thomas More to abort an outstanding career and climb the Tower to the executioner's scaffold? Certainly he did not want it. He was no anarchist. He was a very capable lawyer and lord chancellor in England. He had deep respect for the ordinary law. Robert Bolt places strong words on the lips of More when his son-in-law, William Roper, suggests using his office to arrest Richard Rich as a traitor, spy, and conspirator against him.

> This country's planted thick with laws from coast to coast—man's laws, not God's—and if you cut them down—and you're just the man to do it—d'you think you could stand upright in the winds that would blow then?[2]

[2]Robert Bolt, *A Man for all Seasons* (New York: Random, 1960), p. 66.

But this deep respect for the role of civil law and the need for obedience to it was neither slavish nor bind. He recognized divine laws and the life-giving truth behind them. Again Bolt has More say to his daughter, Margaret, when she came to him in prison to plead for a compromise:

> If we lived in a State where virtue was profitable, common sense would make us good, and greed would make us saintly. And we'd live like animals or angels in the happy land that *needs* no heroes. But since, in fact, we see that avarice, anger, envy, pride, sloth, lust and stupidity commonly profit far beyond humility, chastity, fortitude, justice, and thought, and have to choose, to be human at all . . . why, then, perhaps we *must* stand fast a little—even at the risk of being heroes.[3]

It was More's sense of obedience to a deeper and higher law that kept him from taking the oath of allegiance when almost every bishop in England was willing to do it.

In practically every century of the Church's history, somewhere in the world, Christians have taken similar stands and endured long prison terms, dehumanizing torture or given up their lives. The records of the martyrs speak eloquently of this. Men and women are following in their footsteps today.

It is also significant to note that some of the great theologians (for example, Rahner, de Lubac, Congar, Chenu, Murray, Lyonnet) who influenced the theology adopted by the Vatican II Fathers, were men who knew extended periods of censure or silencing within the Church during their earlier years. Their heroic courage in accepting the restrictions while continuing to study and to serve the truth within the Church eventually led to their own purification and a more mature expression of the truths they sought to emphasize.

Humble, courageous, obedience—embraced in faith—strengthens the inner heart. It moves the person beyond the mediocre and the common. It encourages stretching the human heart to deeper desires and a broader vision. It calls forth the realization that ultimately all of us have a higher call in life that evokes an inner obedience of the whole heart to God.

Vowed obedience

It is historically instructive to note that in the earlier expressions of Christian religious life, obedience was the only one of the three vows which we now ordinarily associate with religious life. The early monks dedicated themselves to a whole way of life and a mission which grew

[3]*Ibid.*, pp. 140-142.

out of stable incorporation in a given community. The vow of obedience introduced them into a new relationship with the abbot and their fellow monks. They accepted a subordinate relationship to their abbot and began to share a common life with all their confreres. The principal details of their consecrated common life were spelled out in the common rule which they accepted as expressive of the way God called them to live an evangelical life.

In religious life, the role of major superiors has usually been clearly enunciated. They are to make God's presence tangible and accessible to the community in the way in which they exemplify, interpret, and ensure the living of the rule of life. They are the symbol of unity. They have the pastoral care of the community. They have to enforce norms when there is carelessness or blatant disregard for them. As superiors, they are called upon to consult with fellow religious about significant decisions. Normally, there is provision for the election or appointment of official consultors for this purpose. But it is also refreshing to note that the classical rule of St. Benedict requires that the abbot call together the whole community when facing more important decisions: "Having heard the advice of the brethren, let him take counsel with himself and then do what he shall judge to be most expedient. Now the reason why we have said that all should be called to counsel, is that God often reveals what is better to the younger."[4]

In this transitional period in the Church, the role of superiors in many religious communities has been weakened. This is undoubtedly due partly to a reaction to the arbitrary authoritarianism which sometimes crept into the role in the past and partly to the temper of the present times. While it is important that real participation be possible on the part of all members, a weakened authority role can lead to very mediocre community life and the reducing of standards of daily behavior to the least common denominator agreed upon by all. Communal discernment may be an especially graced instrument for charting a course at the beginning of an enterprise. Leaving the regulation of daily living to consensus, however, opens the door to selfish individualism in practice. Consensus cannot continue to be reached unless more and more pluralism is accepted. No one is in a strong enough position to insist on the difference between a healthy freedom for individuals and the abuse of freedom in arrogant, selfish, or immoral behavior. Hence, one of the great challenges for the continuing renewal of religious life today is helping the superiors to rediscover in theory and recover in practice the special ministry of leading, guiding, inspiring, teaching, caring, chiding, and especially exemplifying the life of the religious institute.

If we are called to religious life, we will want to recognize how this vow really involves the consecration to a common life. It involves the

[4]Benedict, *The Rule,* chapter 3.

surrender of certain personal freedoms in the interest of a wider and deeper life in common with the brethren. Moreover, the heart of obedience is found in the spirituality which motivates it: a share in Christ's own sacrificial obedience to the Father.

We will want to be particularly sensitive to the need to develop a wholesome practical love which is chastened by the ordinary demands of community life. So much is revealed in either our willingness or our reluctance to sacrifice in the little things of daily living. Obedience in the larger issues of life is directly related to the fostering of an attitude of obedience to the way God leads us to the simple, ordinary duties and circumstances of daily life.

The promise of obedience in diaconate and priesthood

On the day of ordination, each candidate places his hands between those of the ordaining bishop. The bishop then asks each if he is willing to promise his ordinary obedience and respect. When the affirmative response is given, the bishop prays: "May God who began the good work in you bring it to fulfillment."[5]

What is the nature of this obedience for which diocesan candidates prepare? It is grounded ultimately in *sacramental* reality. A man is called by God through the Church to share in the sacrament of Christ's headship over the body of the Church. The ratification of his call comes through the Church, ultimately in the person of the bishop. The man is ordained a deacon or priest through the sacramental ministry of the bishop. Deacons and priests, although they have a ministry in their own right, are ordained as cooperators with the bishop; they share his ministry of sacrament, word, and pastoral charity. Deacons and priests, then, are not independent Church leaders. They participate in the sacramental life and mission of their bishop.

The promise of obedience, then, formally expresses a man's acceptance of this intimate relationship with his bishop. It is not the domestic obedience required by family life or the civil obedience expected of citizens in society or the religious obedience of vowed life. It is an obedience that proclaims a collaborative, but subordinate relationship with the bishop in his three-fold ministry of word, liturgy, and charity.

It means, then, that all ministry of the sacraments or preaching is authentic to the extent that it is entered into in communion with the bishop. The possession of faculties is not merely a juridical reality. It authenticates any public sacramental celebration or proclamation of God's word. It also means that the bishop missions the deacon and

[5]*The New Rite for the Ordination of Deacons, Priests, and Bishops* (Washington, D.C.: USCC Publications, 1968).

priest. He authenticates the specific ministry which they enter into in his diocese. Thus, *self-appointed* sacramental ministry or preaching of the word or special ministries undercut this communion with the bishop and violate the promise of obedience which the deacon or priest has made. Sometimes it will take great courage and strength to remain true to the solemn promise. This may be particularly true if the bishop's approach to his role leaves something to be desired.

In addition to these minimal implications of the promise of obedience, the deacon and priest are called ideally into a close collaborative life and ministry with their bishop. The bishop is both father and brother. As father, he is the sign and promotes the unity among the ordained as well as the whole local Church. His fatherly pastoral care is made present in the local parish through the pastor and his associates. His fatherhood also involves his own communion with his brother bishops and their mutual communion with the bishop of Rome. As brother, he is called to be particularly concerned about the personal life of each priest and deacon. The priest and deacon cannot be passive in this relationship. They are expected to listen to their bishop with their hearts, bring to their bishop suggestions, observations, and assistance, cooperate with him generously, correct him with charity when necessary and truly nurture the bonds of reverence and communion. It is very much in the spirit of their promise of obedience for priests or deacons to take the initiative in strengthening these bonds.

The relationship of lay ministry to ordained ministry

Christians, by virtue of their baptism and confirmation, have a commission to share in Christ's redemptive work in every area of secular life. They witness to God's presence, his love, his desire to be victorious over the powers of evils. God invites them to dedicate themselves and their expertise to extend the reign of Christ into every corner of human life. They *are* the Church in the secular order. Thus, God calls them to be a priestly people (1 Pt. 2:9), offering the spiritual sacrifices (1 Pt. 2:5; Rom. 12:1) of their life and labor to further the work of his kingdom. This is their primary task. In fulfilling it, they enjoy a truly autonomous and redemptive role in this world.

Some lay persons are called to fulfill their task in life in a more explicit relationship to the Church's mission. The enlarging of such possibilities is one of the rich fruits of the Second Vatican Council. In the past, these ministers served for the most part in the teaching, medical, and social-service roles. Now, some are moving more directly into pastoral ministry on college campuses, in parishes, in hospitals, and in spiritual direction centers. The present moment offers us a wonderful opportunity to recognize and nurture the varied gifts of the Holy Spirit for the benefit of the whole Church.

These lay persons, whether members of religious communities or not, find themselves in a two-fold relationship with deacons, priests, and bishops when they enter Church ministry. As members of a pastoral team, they may find themselves in a collaborative relationship with them; as unordained ministers, they are in a sacramentally distinct and subordinate relationship. This means that they will ordinarily be very active participants in pastoral planning and service. But they will not share the sacramentally conferred mission to preach, celebrate the sacraments or govern the local Church. They may participate in decision-making, but may not usurp the ultimate responsibility of bishop or pastor.

This distinction in roles may lead to some awkward situations on the local scene, especially if the ordained leaders are less professional or the lay leaders have a great deal of initiative. But it is good for all to be clear that the ordained role in ordering Church mission is not based on clerical privilege or caste, but on their special sacramental incorporation in Christ's role of headship of the body. We are a sacramental Church, not a secular organization. The close collaboration of lay and religious ministries with those who are ordained should truly strengthen the Church's mission.

Human struggles along the way

As we move toward living and working in a collaborative, yet subordinate relationship with sacramental authority in Church ministry, we undoubtedly will become aware of areas of underdevelopment in ourselves.

First, we want to test our basic capacity to collaborate with others: our peers and persons in authority. We enter into a truly fraternal relationship with our companion Church ministers. A person who cannot work with others will find it very difficult to enter into this kind of fraternal cooperation. Although, as Church ministers we do not commit ourselves to living a common life, we do share a common Church ministry. We cannot, then, see our mission as merely an individual gift. It is an ecclesial gift, given in a special way to the ordained and shared in by those in Church ministry for the sake of all. Individualists who wish to do their own project will find it very difficult to live in communion with their bishop and in fraternity with all who are involved in Church ministry.

Another difficulty may become manifest, paradoxically, in an overly submissive attitude toward authority. There may be almost a rigid compliance with the expectations of authority. We may be very conscientious and cooperative, but lack initiative and self-reliance. We may need to have a tendency toward passive-aggression if we ask a great deal of authority and, then, are captious of them with our peers. It is possible that we may be weak and dependent persons; or we may be angry and withdrawn. In any of these cases, we have not yet matured enough in our relationships with authority to allow for a responsible, adult collaboration in a leadership role. It will be important to address this with a director or counselor to assess our suitability and to receive help.

The more obvious expression of resistance to authority appears in the form of an overly rebellious attitude. We may find ourselves in an ongoing struggle with anyone who makes authoritative demands on us: the director of our training program, a superior, a supervisor. Whenever demands run counter to personal desire, there is conflict. This attitude, too, we want to address with help. If, despite attempts to seek adequate help, we continue without any increased self-insight or interior progress, then we are probably going to be unhappy working in a subordinate relationship and will probably cause much unhappiness for others. It would be better to pursue alternate plans than to allow ourselves to become trapped in a life of inevitable conflict.

While we want to be realistic about facing the obstacles, we want to channel our principal effort into opening up the riches of the spiritual call to obedience. This will undoubtedly mean moving beyond some of the prejudices of our current age to appreciate the mystery of the obedient mind and heart of Christ Jesus.

SHARING IN ECCLESIAL PRAYER

Some of the more moving pictures which the Scriptures bequeath to subsequent generations are those which portray holy men of God in intense intercessory prayer, not for themselves, but for the people. The first that comes to mind is Abraham in dialogue with Yahweh in behalf of the people of Sodom (Gn. 18:16-33). Abraham waited for his companions to leave and then, alone and defenseless, he approached Yahweh and said: "Are you really going to destroy the just man with the sinner?" (Gn. 18:23) Then Abraham proceeded to badger God into a more compassionate stance as if he were bartering with a Near Eastern merchant. There is a largeness of heart and a boldness of spirit that prompts Abraham to risk his friendship with God in interceding for the sinners by drawing God's attention to the plight of the just. This willingness to jeopardize his own favored position and place himself in the middle reveals much of the greatness of Abraham.

A second image is that of Moses, hands raised and supported by Aaron, interceding for his people. Although this particular scene represents Moses' prayer during battle, Moses more often found himself pleading with God after his people had sinned: as at Marah in the desert where the people murmured because of the bitter water they had to drink (Ex. 16:25); in the wilderness of Sin where the people complained for lack of food (Ex. 16: 1-36); at Rephridim where there was no water at all (Ex. 17:4); at the foot of Sinai where the people worshipped a golden calf (Ex. 32:11-14); at Taberah where the people complained bitterly against Yahweh (Nm. 11:10-15); after Miriam and Aaron accused Moses of marrying a foreign woman (Nm. 12:13-14); after the general rebellion against Moses' leadership (Nm. 14:10-19); after the revolt of Korah, Dathan, and Abiram (Nm. 16:4). A meditative reading of the recorded prayers reveals the heart of a man who really sensed himself to be caught between God and his people. Sometimes he was afraid; sometimes he was overwhelmed; sometimes he was angry. He would go to God and put it all before him. Then, in quiet, he would listen and follow God's instructions.

The most powerful image expressing self-immolative intercession to God for the people is that of Jesus, his hands nailed outstretched to embrace all people, the weight of the sins of the whole world bowing his shoulders and head, his parched lips praying: "Father, forgive them; they do not know what they are doing" (Lk. 22:34). The breadth and depth of his sacrificial love for all people and his burning desire to be faithful to the Father's mandate could not know a more dramatic expression than the cross. "During his life on earth, he offered up prayers and entreaty, aloud and in silent tears, to the one who had the power to save him out of death, and he submitted so humbly that his prayer was heard. Although he was Son, he learned to obey through suffering; but, having been made perfect, he became for all who obey him the source of eternal salvation and was acclaimed by God with the title of high priest of the order of Melchizedek (Hb. 5:7-10).

It is the mystery of Jesus' prayer to the Father that the Church tries to appreciate and live. Ecclesial prayer is the Church's way of participating in Christ's prayer.

The prayer of Jesus

The author of the letter to the Hebrews teaches that from the very beginning of his incarnation, Jesus prayed to his Father: "You who wanted no sacrifice or oblation, prepared a body for me. You took no pleasure in holocausts or sacrifices for sin; then, I said—just as I was commanded in the scroll of the book—'God, here I am! I am coming to obey your will' " (Hb. 10:5-7). This prayer seems to reveal so much of the heart of Jesus: his willing acceptance of the Father's mandate; his desire to replace the holocausts of old with the holocaust of himself; his sacrificial love.

The Scriptures go on to testify that Jesus prayed regularly throughout his life. Luke offered a particularly detailed record as he noted that Jesus was at prayer when the Father revealed his mission at his baptism in the Jordan (Lk. 3:21-22); during the whole night before he called the apostles (Lk. 6:12); as he prepared to multiply the loaves (Lk. 9:16); before inviting a confession of faith from Simon Peter (Lk. 9:18); at the top of the mountain where he was transfigured (Lk. 9:28-29); in praise of his Father after the disciples returned from their mission (Lk. 10:21-22).

Jesus' redemptive love was closely connected with daily prayer as he is reported to have gone off to the desert or to a mountain to pray (Mk. 1:35; 6:46; Lk.5:16) or to rise early in the morning (Mk. 1:35) or to remain through the night (Mt. 14:23; Mk.6:46). He is believed to have taken part in the public prayers of the synagogues (Lk. 4:16) and in the temple which he regarded a "house of prayer" (Mt. 21:13). At meal times, he offered the customary blessings as is recorded at the multiplication of loaves (Mt. 14:19), during the Last Supper (Mt. 26:26) and with the two disciples at Emmaus (Lk. 24:30).

Certainly in his passion, Jesus revealed a profound capacity for prayer. As he anticipated his passion, he brought his troubled soul to his Father (Jn. 12:27). During the Last Supper he uttered that extraordinary prayer expressing intimacy with the Father, a desire to be faithful to the end, a redemptive and compassionate love for his followers and all who would come to believe through them and a burning zeal for unity (Jn. 17:1-26). In his agony in the garden, Jesus struggled with the Father's will, poured out his anguish of heart and experienced strengthening grace (Mt. 26:35-44). Even on the cross, Jesus continued to pray for the forgiveness of his murderers (Lk. 23:34), in expression of his intense agony and hope for deliverance (Mt. 27:46) and in surrender of his spirit to the Father (Lk. 23:46).

Christ's prayer was not limited to the time of his earthly sojourn. He is a priest forever. "It follows, then, that his power to save is utterly certain, since he is living forever to intercede for all who come to God through him" (Hb. 7:25). The Church is that body of disciples who continue to come to God through him.

The prayer of the Church

Jesus invited all who were to follow him to the Father to pray. He begged them to pray, to ask, to seek in his name (Jn. 14:13). In response to his disciples' request he taught them the way to pray (Mt. 6:9-13). He insisted that prayer be humble (Lk. 18:9-14), constant (Lk. 21:36), persistent (Lk.18:1-8), authentic (Mt. 6:5-8), and confident in the Father's goodness (Lk. 11:5-13).

The apostles handed on to the Church some of their prayers. They taught others to offer prayers to God through Christ (2 Cor. 1:20; Col. 3:17), in the Holy Spirit (Rm. 8:15). They insisted on praying persistently and attentively (Rm. 12:12).

Thus, the Church from the beginning not only imitated Christ, but joined themselves with him in his prayer (Eph. 5:12). They came together for daily prayer (Acts 2:42). They understood themselves to be a priestly people (1 Pt. 2:9-10), sharing Christ's own life by baptism. They recognized the presence of the Holy Spirit enabling them to pray his words when they knew not what to say (Rm. 8:26).

The Church, over the centuries, has developed and modified a form of prayer which expresses in a special way what the Church is. It is an attempt to help all of us to sense our communion with the Lord Jesus, continuing to offer himself to his Father through the Holy Spirit for the sake of all. The Church gives the psalms a special place because they were such an integral part of Jesus' prayer and because they express so well the variations of human religious experience. The Church also offers a wide selection of readings to help draw us into deeper appreciation of the saving life, death, and resurrection of the Lord and the overall plan of redemption which the Father is still unfolding through him. In response to Christ's admonition to pray always (Lk. 18:1), the Church has shaped this prayer so that it consecrates different times of the day and calls it a Liturgy of the Hours.

In addition to the sanctification of the day, the Church's Liturgy of Hours follows a monthly and yearly rhythm. The psalms are distributed over a four-week span; the temporal and festal cycle follow a yearly and biennial cycle. Thus, not only the hour of the day, but also the days, months, and years enter into sacred time.

All lay people are invited to share in their own way in the Church's prayer. One-volume, abbreviated editions of the Liturgy of Hours are available for those who wish to participate on their own in the prayer of the Church. Deacons and priests are encouraged to invite parishioners into appropriate participation in this prayer. It may be interesting to note that part of the inspiration behind the spread of the rosary was the desire to offer to the laity in the Middle Ages, a way of praying the mysteries celebrated in Church prayer. The one hundred fifty Hail Mary's of the fifteen decades of the rosary took the place of the one hundred fifty psalms of the untranslated Latin psalter for the benefit of the unlettered lay brother or lay people who did not know Latin. Because Mary was the model for all Christians in approaching these mysteries, prayer in union with her was particularly appropriate.

The prayer of the Church, then, should help us to keep our hearts attuned to God, and also foster a rhythm of life which is close to nature. Often, only those who are committed to a stable community life in monasteries can live that to the fullest. Those communities make the praying of the *Opus Dei* their chief ministry. But all of us are invited to share in this rhythm according to the concrete circumstances of our own lives.

Ecclesial prayer in religious communities

From the beginning, religious communities were inspired by the example of the early Jerusalem community described in the Acts of the Apostles (2:42-47; 4:32-35). These communities, which initially were monastic, have normally seen themselves as the Church in miniature composed of members who have come together in support of one another in the deeper living of the Christian life. It was natural for them to want to be the praying Church in as full a way as possible. They introduced a very complete liturgy of prayer which brought together various approaches to Church prayer found in the local Church communities and ultimately gave form to the Liturgy of Hours for the whole Church. In fulfillment of the psalmist's claim, "Seven times daily I praise you . . ." (Ps. 119:16), the monks developed a non-sacramental liturgy which brought them together seven times to pray: matins and lauds, prime, terce, sext, none, vespers, and compline. This last hour of compline emerged first as a dormitory prayer offered as they were retiring. With a simplification in the number of hours and psalms, and a change in some nomenclature, this pattern of prayer is still observed by monks.

In the period of cultural transition from medieval farm life to the emerging city life, St. Francis of Assisi and St. Dominic introduced a model of religious life which still considered the praying of the liturgy of Hours as important, but allowed much more flexibility and mobility in responding to various pastoral needs, especially in the area of good evangelical preaching. The post-reformational period brought further experimentation in a religious life which remained committed to ecclesial prayer, but restricted the common prayer and relegated much of the Liturgy of Hours to private office. This model, embraced by the Society of Jesus, became normative for many new religious communities. The Liturgy of Hours became more private and personal religious exercises became more common. During the present post-Vatican II period, the renewal commission under the direction of the Congregation for Divine Worship has revised the hours and restored a strong emphasis on ecclesial prayer. As yet, this aspect of renewal is not as fully appreciated as it might be.

During formation, therefore, religious want to learn how to enter into the Liturgy of Hours intelligently and with faith. They need adequate instruction not only in the history and significance of ecclesial prayer, but also in the understanding of the psalms and biblical history. This instruction is not primarily for educational purposes, but to lead the candidates into biblical prayer. Thus, this training should facilitate an appropriate understanding of history, biblical context, hermeneutics and exegesis as background for meeting God through the text in prayer. It should lead the candidates to a respect for the liturgical texts as a school of prayer. Candidates can learn to acquire new insights and enter into deeper movements of the heart as they pray these texts regularly. In fact, the candidate's willingness to be drawn into deeper reflection and more absorbing prayer by the Church's texts will lead beyond pettiness and myopia both in prayer and in life.

The Liturgy of Hours and those who are ordained

If the foregoing is understood, then the priest's commitment to a daily praying of the Liturgy of Hours makes eminent sense. The Church law which requires this commitment is not arbitrary or extrinsic to the priesthood. Just as all Christians are called to become a praying Church, so the ordained leaders of the Church are called to become leaders of a praying Church. The Acts of the Apostles portrays the nascent Church as persevering in prayer. The apostles instituted the order of deacon so that they themselves could remain faithful to the ministry of prayer and the word (Act 6:4). Paul repeatedly mentioned his own prayer, urged the people to prayer and summoned them to pray with him and for him.

Intrinsic, then to leadership in the Church is experience in prayer and the capacity to lead others. This is not a mere formalism. People need to be helped by priests who have really become men of prayer. Otherwise, priests will actually become an obstacle to interior life among the faithful.

Cornelia Jessey writes in a recent article[1] of the moving religious journey of the English writer, Rosamond Lehmann.[2] She seemed to experience mystical intuition especially when she faced shocking suffering. But, because she had memories only of external and formal preaching and counsel from the clergy in her church, she never thought to turn to them for interpretation, guidance and encouragement.

In another instance, the teacher of a high-school religion class recently invited a guest to come in to talk to the teenagers about prayer. The youngsters became very interested and intrigued with the possibilities of prayer. When the suggestion was made that they might get help in prayer from their parish priests, the faces of the youngsters registered surprise. One girl blurted out: "I never thought to go to one of them. I thought they just took care of the Masses and ran the parish."

The responsibility to help people in the life of prayer is integral to ordained priesthood. It presumes a growing depth on the part of the seminarian and the priest. It also presumes a special kind of formation nourished by the Scriptures and the Church's spiritual tradition. That is why the revised office of readings offers such an extensive, systematic exposure to the Scriptures and a significantly increased selection of writings from the spiritual tradition. So many young people today turn to non-Christian spirituality principally because no one has opened up for them the riches of the Christian spiritual tradition.

Candidates for ordained priesthood will want to grow into an appreciation of the Liturgy of Hours. Because priests in the past have frequently approached the praying of their breviary rather formalistically and a number in the post-Vatican II era have given up this prayer altogether, the seminarian may not have many good models to follow. They will need help in working through some of the same questions mentioned above for religious. But the diocesan priest will not ordinarily find himself praying the Liturgy of Hours with a community. This can be a real handicap. It will take stronger motivation to keep faithful in a meaningful way. The Church recognizes morning and evening prayer as central. The priest should not normally have any reason to disregard that responsibility. Moreover, his meditative reading of the office of

[1]"Mystics without Portfolio," *Desert Call* (Winter, 1977), pp. 13-17.

[2]Rosamond Lehman describes this herself in *The Swan in the Evening, Fragments of an Inner Life.*

readings is the Church's way of leading him into *lectio divina* and a greater familiarity with the basic spiritual tradition. This is so important for his preaching and teaching as well as his own spiritual nourishment. Finally, the mid-day prayer and night prayer will provide a graced opportunity for lifting the heart to God at noon and before retiring.

Permanent deacons are invited, but not obligated to a daily praying of the Liturgy of Hours. They are incorporated in the three-fold ministry of the Church in word, liturgy, and charity. Like the original deacons, their special focus of service is on the extension of the ministry of pastoral charity so that priests may be more free for prayer and service to the word (Acts 6:3).

In some living situations, it may be possible for priests and deacons to join one another in a portion of this prayer. The Church considers morning and evening prayer the central hour which takes precedence over all others.

Because this prayer belongs to the whole Church, the priest will want to assist the laity in praying some portions of the Liturgy of Hours in a way that is helpful to them. Paraliturgical services, prayers in connection with parish meetings and other occasions for devotional services could provide possible settings. A priest may simply invite the people to join in the praying of a single psalm at first, the scriptural reading and the concluding prayer. What is important is the way in which it is done and the sense given the people that they are truly joining in the prayer of the Church. This involvement of some of the people in the Church's prayer can strengthen and deepen his own commitment.

It is the Spirit that prays in Christians

The bane of organized religion is formalism. Merely external prayer (Mt. 6:5), or merely external religious observance (Mt.6:1) robs our own religion of its inner life and deters others from finding God. Formalism sabotages true faith.

This is why Jesus promised that he would enable his disciples to worship "in spirit and in truth" (Jn. 4:23-24). He would send the Holy Spirit to lead them to a fuller understanding both of the Father and of Jesus (Jn. 16:13-14). This Spirit "comes to help us pray in our weakness. For when we cannot choose words in order to pray properly, the Spirit himself expresses our plea in a way that could never be put into words, and God who knows everything in our hearts knows perfectly well what we mean, and that the pleas of the saints expressed by the Spirit are according to the mind of God" (Rm.8:26-27).

There are real advantages to allowing the Spirit through the Church to put the words on our lips in the Liturgy of Hours. Creative self-expression has all the limitations of the person who is trying to pray. The Church's prayer touches the full spectrum of human religious emotion and experience. Personal immersion in this more universal prayer catapults the timid heart into a solidarity with the joys and sufferings, hopes and disappointments, love and anger of all people.

The Spirit not only suggests the words, but also dwells in the heart and facilitates inner involvement in the prayer. This frees the inhibited self and opens up the horizons of God's transcendent mystery. The initiation to transcendence treated in the first part of this book has special relevance for praying the Liturgy of Hours with the heart. The movement beyond mere managerial control of life's responsibilities and the enlivened sense of the beautiful, the life-giving, the true, the holy, and the transcendent direct us to prayer in the Spirit.

One caution may be introduced here in an age of creative self-expression. The goal of prayer is neither undisciplined spontaneity nor elaborate self-expression. It is self-transcendence, worship, the gift of one's whole life in love. The Liturgy of Hours is an extension of Eucharistic spirituality. Thus, the prayer of the Church follows the Eucharistic paradigm by helping us to take the bread of the Church's sacred words, to bless God with them, to break them and give them to others with the bread of our own lives. This is the kind of involvement in prayer that the Spirit makes possible. This is praying "in spirit and in truth" (Jn. 4:23-24).

Good ecclesial prayer is not easy

Church ministers are called to become persons of prayer, nourished by the Scriptures and the spiritual tradition for the sake of the people. This is not an easy goal. Good prayer requires serious work. And there are many difficulties that we can face along the way.

First, we may be tempted to view our commitment to prayer as Church ministers as basically no different than any other Christian's. There is a sense in which this is true. Since all are called to holiness, so all are called to prayer. But the role of leaders of prayer is different. This is especially true of priests who are called to be ordained leaders of prayer, teachers of prayer, and guides of prayer. Hence, by sacramental ordination they are formally deputed by the whole Church to become true men of Church prayer. Religious, on the other hand, by virtue of profession, freely choose to enter in a special way into the Liturgy of Hours to express more fully what the prayer of the Church is and can be. What ordinary people are not so able to do in this regard, the religious does in union with them and their needs. So, if we are candidates for ordination or religious life and fail to want this or even fight ecclesial prayer, we are missing an essential ingredient of the life.

Secondly, some of us may be inclined to construct our own common prayer *ex nihilo*. Our educational orientation may have been toward creative self-expression. We rightly recognize that God speaks to people in many different ways; in creation, in secular literature, in film, in contemporary music. This can be very helpful for special para-liturgical services. But men and women of *ecclesial* prayer create a profoundly personal response out of givens: the Scriptures, classical spiritual literature, liturgical texts. In this they look to the reformed Liturgy of Hours as normative. Wisdom dictates that clerical and religious candidates have to appreciate and accept that before moving on to a final commitment.

Lastly, some of us will be tempted to view the Liturgy of Hours as our sole expression of prayer. We may not yet have entered into self-transcendent prayer. The use of the prayer of the Church can become for us a way of praying without truly meeting God and his transforming love. The formula prayer becomes a convenient defense against real personal engagement. It is easier to say prayers than to become adult men and women of prayer. This leads to the formalism that undermines true faith—one's own and that of others.

All of these possible stumbling blocks suggest the need for spiritual guidance. Only those who pray with their hearts, can pray well in a life of pastoral charity.

EMBRACING PASTORAL CHARITY

Graham Greene has an uncanny gift for tracing the power of God's grace in quite inadequate human instruments, especially priests. In *The Power and the Glory,* a nameless priest is pursued by an anonymous lieutenant of police in the state of Tabasco in southern Mexico during the Communist persecutions of the Church in the nineteen-thirties. He is also pursued by God. This hapless whiskey priest who knows in humiliating fashion the weakness of his own flesh, is neverthelèss able to keep alive some semblance of faith when he is finally captured and brought before the rigidly self-disciplined Communist lieutenant. Greene has him say to the lieutenant:

> That's another difference between us. It's no good your working for your end unless you're a good man yourself. And there won't always be good men in your party. Then you'll have all the old starvation, beating, get-rich-anyhow. But it doesn't matter so much my being a coward—and all the rest. I can put God into a man's mouth just the same—and I can give God's pardon. It wouldn't make any difference to that if every priest in the Church was like me.[1]

These words seems to come from the priest, not as a self-defense, but as an act of faith that God far transcends humankind and its weaknesses. In much of his writing, Greene seems to be preoccupied with this hidden and persistent presence of God which continues to redeem in the most unlikely of circumstances. Here he draws attention to the truth that God's saving work through priests mercifully does not depend utterly on their personal integrity. God can save through imperfect instruments; he can even save this imperfect instrument, a whiskey priest.

Although *The Power and the Glory* illustrates this profound truth, Greene does not exonerate priests of their responsibilities. In *A Burnt-Out Case,* Greene obviously considers Father Thomas' smug theories about sin, grace, and virtue quite inadequate and even inane as an explanation for the redemptive mystery of grace being slowly and victoriously worked out in the gradual transformation of the burnt-out Querry. God's transcendent redemptive power is real, but it does not excuse his priests of their responsibility to do their part. Green's novels, then, suggest a two-fold truth: God can save anyone through anyone he wants; yet, God still asks that his Church ministers try to live what they

[1]Graham Greene, *The Power and the Glory* (New York: Viking Press, 1970), pp. 262-263.

preach. This chapter is about trying to live the Christian message in pastoral care.

Jesus as pastor

To express this special kind of care, the Scriptures often use the agrarian image of pastor. It is the image of the shepherd tending his sheep. Early in the Old Testament, Yahweh was called the Shepherd of Israel (Gn. 44:24; 48:15). Yahweh is the shepherd who goes before his flock (Ps. 68:7), who guides it (Ps. 23:3), who leads it to pastures (Jer. 50:19), and to restful places near water (Ps. 23:6), who protects it with his staff (Ps. 23:4) and who gathers the dispersed (Is. 56:8).

Because the human shepherds of Israel had become unfaithful, Yahweh was to visit them (Jer. 2:8; Ez. 34:1-10). He himself was to take over the office of shepherd and gather and feed the scattered flock (Jer.23:3; Ez. 34:11-22). First he would be their shepherd through David (Ez. 34:23). But-eventually the one who would be the shepherd would fulfill a mysterious suffering role (Zech. 13:7). Thus, at the end of the Old Testament development of the shepherd theme, there is an intimation that the shepherd would suffer death as part of God's plan for the salvation of his people.

Jesus referred to himself as the messianic shepherd promised in the Old Testament (Jn. 10:11). He used the image to describe his mission of gathering the dispersed flock (Mt.15:24). He also used the figure to intimate to his disciples his death and return (Mk. 14:27). The shepherd became part of his illustration of the drama of the last judgment (Mt. 25:31-46). In the parable of the good shepherd (Jn. 10:1-30), Jesus contrasted the good shepherd with the thief, the hireling, and the stranger. He identified himself with the good shepherd who lays down his life for his sheep (Jn. 10:11).

Perhaps, it is possible to appreciate this shepherd theme more if we ponder the unique relationship which seems to exist between the oriental shepherd and his flock. The sheep, gentle and defenseless, seem to possess an instinctive sense that they can trust the shepherd to lead them out to nourishing pastures. A good shepherd moves toward noon to the richest, shadiest spot near running water so that the sheep can continue to eat while being sheltered from the scorching sun and refreshed by the moving water. Sometimes during this noonday relaxation, individual sheep will move out of formation to come over to the shepherd. He will call them by name and reassure them by his caress. This scene suggests a moving intimacy between sheep and shepherd. The sheep rely on the shepherd's crook to snatch them out of briars or from the craggy rocks if they slip far below. The shepherd has to ward off wild dogs or other predatory animals with his staff. At the end of the day, he checks each for wounds and then anoints the wounds that he finds with oil as a healing balm. The sheep then sleep in security.

This image of the good shepherd suggests much of the Lord's faithful caring presence to all his people. It bespeaks intimate relationship, trust, protection, guidance, nourishment, healing, and care. This pastoral love Jesus showers on each disciple; he also calls some disciples to image it to others in a public Church ministry.

Pastoring in the Church

Paul was the first theologian in the Church. In one of his reflections on the Church as the unified Body of Christ, he noted that Jesus sent the Spirit after his glorification to distribute different gifts of calls in the Church. Among the various calls is the one of shepherding or pastoring (Eph. 4:11). Luke records that Paul in bidding farewell to the presbyters at Ephesus had said: "Be on your guard for yourselves and for all the flock of which the Holy Spirit has made you overseers, to feed the Church of God which he bought with his own blood. I know quite well that when I am gone fierce wolves will invade you and will have no mercy on the flock" (Acts 20:28-29). The use of this image to describe Jesus' continuing care exercised through special leaders in the Church echoes Jesus' own post-resurrectional dialogue with Simon Peter on the shores of the Sea of Galilee. Three times Jesus invited him to profess his love for the Lord; three times Simon Peter responded affirmatively as if repenting for his three-fold denial; three times Jesus uttered the words commissioning him to shepherd his lambs or his sheep (Jn. 21:15-17). Peter evidently did not interpret this role as belonging to him alone, for he later wrote: "Now I have something to tell your elders: I am an elder myself, and a witness to the sufferings of Christ, and with you I have a share in the glory that is to be revealed. Be the shepherds of the flock of God that is entrusted to you . . ." (1 Pt. 5:1-2).

The role of pastoring involves guarding the flock (1 Pt. 5:2; 2 Tim. 3:1-17), humble service (1 Pt. 5:3), leading by example (1 Pt. 5:3), protecting the people from false teachers (1 Tim.1:3-7; 4:1-16; 2 Tim. 2:14-26; Tit. 1:10-16), handing on the message faithfully (1 Tim.1:18-25; 6:2-10; 2 Tim. 4:1-5; Tit. 2:1-3:8), leading the people in prayer (1 Tim. 2:1-8), exercising a genuine care for the needs of different people (1 Tim. 5:1-6:2; 6:17-19), being willing to face hardships (2 Tim.2:1-13).

This ministry of pastoring in God's Church is not self-initiated. It is God who extends the invitation. "You did not choose me; no, I chose you and I commissioned you to go out and to bear fruit, fruit that will last (Jn. 15:16). God gives the call as an inner desire which is then brought to the Church for testing and refining. "No one takes this

honor on himself, but each one is called by God, as Aaron was"
(Hb.5:4).

Incorporation in ordained ministry

Some members of the Church are called to enter into the ordained
shepherding ministry. Bishops in union with the bishop of Rome share
in this in a pre-eminent way. But all who enter holy orders are
sacramentally configured to Christ in his shepherding role. This
sacramental configuration is more than the conferal of a shepherd's
role. It involves the reorienting of the whole person, enabling the ordained to act *in persona Christi* and effectively to continue Christ's
presence in sacrament in the Church and in the world. Bishops, priests,
and deacons share in the role according to their rank and sacramental
power. Together they form a *collegium*. Their mission is to sacramentalize Christ's continuing presence in his Church through a ministry of
word, liturgy, and pastoral charity. Since ordination is a grace given for
the upbuilding of the entire body of Christ, all the ordained are considered co-shepherds living and working with their local bishops and in
communion ultimately with the bishop of Rome.

Hence, it behooves candidates for ordination to recognize that they
are professing an intention to enter a life which will touch their whole
being very profoundly. They are embracing more than an interesting
way to spend their lives. Their whole lives will be caught up in God.
This is why the Church has considered celibacy to be a particularly appropriate way to express this truth. For in ordination, a man is affected
in the very depths of his being, even though it will take a life-time to
come to appreciate and live this special configuration to Christ. Beyond
this in-depth reorientation of life, the ordained will be entering a collaborative life and ministry. Hence, the Church asks an acceptance of
the sacramental bonds to bishop, priests, and deacons.

The unique life of the ordained calls for special areas of ascetical
discipline. In addition to those already treated—celibate consecration,
simplicity of life, an obedient collaboration and a vibrant life of prayer
in the Church—the ordained shepherds are called to a special concern
for continuing study and the development of the art of pastoring.

The study of theology and the allied disciplines is much more than
just a preparation for ordination. Candidates for ordination are not ordinarily preparing for an academic career. But they are entering into a
life that will require serious, sustained reading and reflection on the
faith realities and their meaning for the people. They, therefore, want
to develop the capacity for disciplined, intelligent, and faith-inspired
thought. This virtue is not superoragatory. It is an intrinsic part of a
responsible spiritual life for the ordained. It is a virtue which enables

them to enter into a much more responsible ministry of charity to those who are confused about faith or morals, those who are seeking enlightenment and those who find themselves facing complex decisions in life.

Candidates for ordination are also preparing for caring service to others. It is important to take any field assignments seriously. There is a wisdom to limiting the hours of field involvement to a necessary minimum. The accent in field education should not be on the multiplication of experiences or even on the development of skills for ministry. These emphases can consume a great deal of time and energy without concomitant growth in the candidates. It is far better to have a rather limited involvement coupled with concurrent in-depth reflection. The reflection can then help them to interpret and evaluate their experience in a way that leads to deeper life. Otherwise, the personal self-knowledge, self-acceptance, repentance, conversion of heart and consequent compassion for others that are tremendously important resources for ordained ministry can be lost sight of in the draining pace of personal involvement in the lives of others.

Participating in Church Ministry

Although the New Testament ordinarily restricts the shepherding image to Jesus himself and then extends it by analogy only to the apostles, overseers, and presbyters, it is, nevertheless, true by further analogy that other ministers in the Church participate in some way in a shepherding role. In particular, Paul's close association of the shepherds with the teachers (Eph.4:11) seems to suggest this possibility.

Even if the shepherding role is interpreted more restrictively, there is no doubt that the New Testament Church recognized and endorsed other forms of leadership and ministry in the Church (Rm.12:3-8; 1 Cor.12:4-30). Paul described them as gifts of the Spirit to the Church (1 Cor.12:4) which form the one Body of Christ (1 Cor.12:12-13). The Church needs all of them (1 Cor.12:14-21). In fact, the least significant in man's eyes may be the most important (1 Cor.12:22-26). There is, however, an ordering of these gifts for the sake of unity (1 Cor.12:27-30; 14:26-40; Eph.4:4-6).

These diverse gifts ground a variety of ministries (1 Cor.12:4), so that some are called to be apostles, prophets, evangelists, pastors, and teachers (Eph.4:11). There is no reason to interpret Paul's listing as taxative. The Church at different times has further specified this list with acolytes, lectors, catechists, exorcists, porters, directors of music. The ordained ministry has an important charge to foster these various gifts.

Even though the functions differ with each gift, all are called to the higher gift—charity (1 Cor.12:31-13:13). The various offices in the Church are intended to build together the Body of Christ (Eph.4:12).

However, persons who receive these gifts *for* the Church can regretfully use them *against* the Church. It is charity that binds the Church together. It is charity which is the basis of each of the ministries.

Candidates in apostolic religious communities will want to discover how their particular ministry relates to the whole Body. There is an inner joy in discovering the nobility of one's specific role while recognizing humbly its relationship to the whole. This discovery is closely linked to an ever deeper appreciation of the mystery of the Church in which the religious is an active and significant participant.

Religious and all lay leaders will also need to address some of the practical issues of responsible collaboration with ordained leaders and humble, detached service to those in need. It is important that unity and compassion mark Church ministry.

There are two special gifts to the Church which have increased in importance in recent years. They are the ministry of spiritual direction and ministry to social justice.

Some may be called to the deeper ministry of spiritual direction. It is an area of ministry that many seem to avoid. It is good to be hesitant about touching such a profoundly personal area of another's life. A wholesome hesitance opens the way for a more respectful approach.

In a general sense, much of Church ministry is spiritual direction. It involves helping others to find their way to God in this world either in a direct or indirect way. As Church ministers, we want to serve God's word wherever it is to be found in life.

Those who are called to ordained priesthood have a unique opportunity to do this. They can enter into preaching and teaching of God's word in such a way that they facilitate an inner hearing and responding to it. They can celebrate sacramental life in such a way that people are drawn to enter into the mysteries and live them more fully in their lives. They can lead public prayer in such a way that people are attracted to participate interiorily themselves. They can approach various pastoral situations with a great sensitivity for the things of the spirit.

Some, whether ordained or not, may be gifted to help others personally in discerning and responding to God in their lives. These should not be self-appointed spiritual guides, but trusted men and women whose wisdom and understanding of the ways of God spontaneously invite others to test their inner life with them. When this happens, they receive a sacred trust. It demands on their part deep reverence for the person, wise knowledge of the fundamentals of Christian spiritual life, the inner strength to state what needs to be said and the compassion to allow for the gradual nature of the spiritual journey of another. This kind of approach usually depends most on a growing interior appreciation of their own journey in faith. Whenever a person is going to move into this role in a more specialized way, those responsible ought to provide for appropriate training.

Another area of pastoral care which is sometimes ignored is concern for the larger societal issues of peace and justice. No one can be involved in everything. But the heart of a true Church minister must be expansive. The priest has to be realistic about tangible commitments. However, there will be social dimensions to the authentic proclamation of the gospel, sacramental celebration and pastoral care of the people. His may be the most important voice in broadening vision, heightening awareness of injustice, and in encouraging people to respond to any call which they may receive to work in this area in a truly Christian way. It is a great challenge to present and interpret the Church's social teaching with a sense of urgency, but without reducing it to any secularistic ideology.

Some religious or other lay ministers may have a more explicit call to a social ministry. This ministry may involve the personal care of individual people or concern for larger societal issues. Both are important vocations in the Church. Just as in every other area of pastoral care, those who enter this ministry must keep alive the basic spiritual dimensions to their lives. The problems and struggles that confront such generous people are enormous. It is easy to be overwhelmed and feel powerless. Resentment not only against unjust social structures, but also against God who permits these to perdure can build. Soon the temptation is to assume God's role, since he sometimes seems to be doing so badly by himself. The minister can begin to struggle for a secular redemption and lose sight of the transcendent. Dedicated workers who can be inwardly faithful to their own communion with God, conversion of heart and the primacy of sacrificial charity in their lives will ultimately be the more fruitful mediators of God's redemptive grace.

Pastoral care

No matter what may be our specific ministry, we will want to be solicitous to strengthen the spiritual dimensions of true pastoral ministry. Individuals who want to help others can sometimes do more harm than good. All of the areas of spiritual formation touched upon thus far have a bearing on pastoral care. For instance, if we are not open to a transcendent God and have not experienced some real communion with God, we will tend to avoid ministry to the human spirit. If we have very limited self-knowledge or entered into little or no personal conversion, then unfaced neuroses or sinfulness can sabotage the pastoral relationship. If we have not moved beyond self-serving patterns of love, we will be inclined to reach out to others more to satisfy personal needs than to discern and respond to the real needs of others. If we are not true ecclesial men or women, we may find it very difficult to help others discover the true mystery of the Church. If we have no clear personal, sexual, or vocational identity, we can lose ourselves in our effort to help others.

Thus, as we enter into pastoral care, we need to keep on the journey of spiritual conversion. Ample time for solitude is a necessity. Care for others is draining and tends to diffuse human energies and resources. Quiet time allows for the space and opportunity for prayer, reflection on experience, growth in self-knowledge, the emergence of humility before God and the growing sense that it is God who really does the caring. This kind of tranquil refreshment strengthens a wholesome respect for oneself and a desire to foster and protect respect for others. It becomes possible to move away from manipulative or egocentric tendencies. It diminishes the power of those unrefined competitive drives which lead to harsh and unfeeling attempts to prove self or outplay others in the service of the needy.

Genuine pastoral care is expressive of warm hospitality. This is the virtue which allows us to be receptive and welcoming without being superficial. Only if we have a center within ourselves and room in our inner home for others can we truly make others feel welcome in our presence. An unfeigned, welcoming smile can, then, sacramentalize a heart that truly cares, yet grants to the visitor utter freedom to come or go.

Obviously, then, pastoring is not simply a functional role. It is more than all the various services that may be involved in good pastoral ministry. First and foremost, pastoring is a participation in Christ's sacrificial love for others. The shepherd is to be consecrated in love to the Lord. It is significant to note that Jesus gave his mission to Simon Peter only after he elicited from him a three-fold expression of love for him (Jn.21:15-17). Paul, the zealous evangelizer and pastor, experienced a profound identification in love with Jesus: "I have been crucified with Christ, and I live now not with my own life, but with the life of Christ who lives in me" (Gal. 2:19-20). It is this personal love for Jesus and the willingness to lay down our lives for others (Jn. 10:11) that is at the heart of pastoral charity. Moved in gratitude for the gifts of nature and grace we have received, we are drawn to want to share in Christ's redemptive love for others.

This desire to love even to the point of sacrifice is the road to humble leadership. Arrogance in a Church leader is repulsive. Church leaders today live in a very sophisticated world. If they propose simplistic approaches to quite complex human problems, they may effectively exclude themselves from fruitful ministry to others. The secular world needs wisdom rather than arrogant interpretations of the world's problems. There is need of a humble, yet firm approach. It ought to flow from inner strength. For sometimes it is going to call for courageous stands that may lead to public ridicule, harassment and in some areas of the world, torture, imprisonment, or death. Walter Ciszek in his book, *He Leadeth Me,* describes movingly the long, uneven struggle he experienced in trying to reconcile the most humiliating of circumstances in Soviet concentration camps with the inner courage to be true to principle. Paradoxically, it was when he most seemed to fail that God saved him and truly made him strong.[2]

Stumbling blocks to pastoral charity

Thus, pastoral charity requires a significant degree of oblative love—the capacity to live for God and others. Inevitably, we will find stumbling blocks as we reach out toward this graced way of living.

Some of us, for instance, may have been attracted to Church ministry because we sensed a less competitive atmosphere, greater freedom of movement without rigorous accountability, and wider opportunities to experience acceptance in a public way. This can be a serious handicap if we enjoy little self-acceptance. We may need to manipulate our environment to receive the support and acclaim that gives us some self-respect. The more we are victims of this tendency, the more risk there will be for us. It usually means limited inner life because we find it frightening to stop, look, and listen. We will probably tend to enter into a hurried pace of life, moving quickly from situation to situation, afraid of in-depth and sustained encounter. In the early years of Church ministry, we may be able to arrange things sufficiently to win considerable acclaim and applause. We will work hard and try new things. The test will emerge when people begin to take us for granted or when we meet considerable disagreement or opposition. We may limit our ministry to those who support us. Or we may be inclined to dismiss the people in the local situation and to start again some place else. This contributes to a pattern of running away from self-confrontation. In recent years, the opportunity to perpetuate this pattern has been increased by the greater flexibility and mobility usually permitted in personnel assignments. Sometimes the running includes leaving priesthood, religious life, or marriage.

We will probably need help in detecting the signs of this behavior. We may be unable to spend much of any time alone. We may always seem to have pressing demands which crowd out quiet time. We may be involved in a number of projects for others. If we are talented, we may even be labeled an effective an involved leader. But inwardly, we are running scared. We have great difficulty entering the spirit world, communing with God or entering into conversion of heart. This has to be faced or we should not continue to a final commitment.

Another situation exists when we build a wall around ourselves to

[2]Walter Ciszek with Daniel Flaherty, *He Leadeth Me* (New York: Doubleday, 1973).

limit human interaction. We may be shy and retiring. We will be aloof in ministry. Church ministry will become a way of lending credibility and social acceptance to anti-social behavior. Our spirituality will be defensive and private. We will have little sympathy for social issues or involvement. We will tend to limit ourselves to a bare minimum in personal service to others.

In the early period of preparation, this pattern should be recognizable because we will tend to arrange our life to minimize ordinary human contact. We may avoid meaningful involvement in field education. We may live a good deal of our life in our own safe enclaves. We may avoid participation in group activities. We may order our day to protect outselves from much informal contact with others. Refusal to accept help or the inability to move out of this pattern raises serious questions about our suitability for any ministry to other people.

The pastoral care of others as Gregory the Great suggests in his *Cura Pastoralis* is the art of arts.[3] It is a great gift from God. To enter into the practice of this art fruitfully is a work of grace. The practitioner is an instrument of God. Like Graham Greene, St. Paul believed in the ultimate triumph of God's grace no matter how weak the instrument. "It is all God's work. It was God who reconciled us to himself through Christ and gave us the work of handling on this reconciliation" (2 Cor.4:18). Like Graham Greene and Gregory the Great, St. Paul also knew that the Church minister has to face himself before God: "I treat my body hard and make it obey me, lest after preaching to others, I myself should be disqualified" (1 Cor. 9:27).

---

[3]Gregory the Great, *Pastoral Care,* Henry Davis, tr. (Westminster, Md: Newman Press, 1950), Part I, chapter 1, p. 21.

A Practical Guide To Spiritual Formation

CONCLUSION

HELPING OTHERS PREPARE FOR CHURCH MINISTRY

This book is an attempt to express what is central to spiritual formation for Church ministry in the Catholic tradition. Although it is primarily addressed to those who seek to prepare for or are already engaged in Church ministry, it may be appropriate in this final chapter to treat some issues which affect those who exercise a formational role. This includes spiritual directors in seminaries, spiritual directors of candidates in a training program for the permanent diaconate and formation directors in programs training religious or laity for Church ministry. In an analogous way, it includes the formation personnel of any apostolic religious community.

Formation work is probably one of the most difficult ministries in the Church. It involves us intimately in the lives of others. It is a hidden work. What is most worthwhile in the work transpires in the silence of the candidates' hearts or in the simple, undramatic day to day interaction which we may have with the candidates. Few understand the nature of the work. Someone very close to me continues to regard this work as the easiest of ministries: "All you have to do is to sit there, listen, and then tell them what to do." Others will volunteer unsolicited advice such as: "Be sure and toughen them up." Most do not appreciate how self-consciously young people deal with issues which a generation ago we took for granted: sexual identity, Christian faith, membership in the Catholic Church, and vocational decision. Superiors may be especially concerned about the external performance of candidates; peers may offer us advice based on their memories of their own experiences in training; the candidates themselves often resent some restrictive or evaluative aspects of any formation experience. Undoubtedly, the heaviest burden we carry as formation directors is the responsibility to offer an evaluative judgment in helping candidates to determine the authenticity of God's call. It is not surprising that few directors remain in a formational role for an extended period of time. Yet, wisdom emerges only after extended experience has been reflected on in faith. It seems important, then, to select directors carefully and to offer them suitable training.

The ministry of spiritual formation

As directors of a formation program, our first task usually involves helping the candidates enter a new way of life. Our role in this regard will vary tremendously, depending on the nature of the program and the candidates. Religious novitiates will ordinarily offer the most extended space and time structured for this purpose; diocesan seminaries will require a mixture of a semi-controlled environment during the academic year and unstructured time during vacation periods; ministry training programs do not usually offer a structured living experience, but will ordinarily insist on personal spiritual direction and a short retreat. No matter what the setting is, we will want to help the candidates find a rhythm of life which includes the ingredients already treated in the chapter, "Growing Communion with God." The bones of any progràm, usually including morning and evening prayer, meditative reading and personal prayer, regular participation in the Eucharist and a periodic approach to the sacrament of reconciliation, need to be enlivened by the spirit of faith, hope, and love.

In leading others into the structures which facilitate deeper life, we are interested in nurturing faith-life. Structures, like the bones of the human body, provide an external form and permit the life within to emerge and express itself more vibrantly. But the bones are not the life itself. The goal of structures is *order* to promote greater integration. Candidates will need considerable help in organizing their lives in such a way that their various involvements and responsibilities serve a unified life. Order does not guarantee faith-life. But it can serve and facilitate it.

In helping candidates into a spiritual way of life, instruction will be very important. The following of the Lord involves embracing a way of life that frees a person to hear Jesus' teaching with the heart. The realities touched on in this book need to be treated in any program. A public expression of the spiritual teaching contributes to an atmosphere which supports individual efforts and also suggests areas for more personal dialogue in spiritual direction. What spiritual reading is for the individual, public spiritual conferences are for the group.

It would be a mistake for us to approach the instructional sessions as if they were lectures. The purpose of these public sessions is not to teach a course in spirituality, but to touch on the ordinary human struggles in trying to appropriate the life-giving truths of faith. It is important to cultivate an atmosphere which is open to God's inspiration. We have to move beyond any desires to impose ourselves or impress others; candidates have to set aside any tendencies to analyze and criticize rather than to receive graced insight with gratitude. A student once approached me after a conference to point out how the atmosphere had changed dramatically when I entertained challenging questions from the group. Prayerful receptivity had suffered; an engaging debate had ensued. The spiritual conference is not the time for such exchange. It is better to provide another forum for this kind of dialogue. We want to foster a climate in the spiritual conference which encourages both director and directees to seek God's light in understanding the road to spiritual life.

Similarly, retreats are special moments in life when the managerial style of life is set aside for a more sustained opening of ourselves to God in prayer. Retreats are formative, not primarily because they offer special insight or inspiration, but because they help to train us in becoming more quiet in soul, in listening to God more attentively with the heart and in responding to God more fully with our whole lives. If retreat time offers only a moment for human relaxation or an intense religious experience, it does not truly help us to live our ordinary lives much better. The life of charity has far more to do with living the ordinary well. We will probably have to resist considerable pressure at times to keep the retreat programs from being diverted from their purpose.

In addition to the spiritual program offered to an entire group, there is the central role of personal spiritual direction. The best structures in the world can be deadening, if personal interior life is not being fostered and guided. We will want to insist on each candidate receiving competent spiritual direction from among those specially designated for this work. Those who are selected for such a role should be screened carefully and should be expected to work closely with the formation director. They should be the kind of person who arouses confidence and trust, gives evidence of wisdom and maturity in daily life, can enter into a contemplative presence with God, others, and life in general and is able to uncover the deeper meaning of the Church's doctrine and discipline.

Personal spiritual direction is an art. Every human art presumes a fundamental giftedness. But art also demands discipline and refinement. We are going to want to listen attentively to each candidate and to the expectations of the Church. We will often find ourselves struggling to be faithful both to the unique way in which God may be leading an individual candidate and the objective demands of a particular Church ministry which the candidate may want to enter. It is a challenge to be utterly true to someone's uniquely personal journey with its invitations to gradual self-knowledge and transformation while helping to unfold in an objective way the Church's expectations for a given role. We want to help the candidates clarify and respond to their own inner life direction in honest dialogue with the real possibilities. Candidates need to sense that we want to help them truly to find God's call in the concrete. Humility, wisdom, and inner strength will inspire confidence. Sincere faith will be important for both director and directee.

One of the principal aims of personal spiritual direction in a formation experience is the discernment of personal vocation. As already noted, this is a crucial and delicate task. Because this involves such important judgments for us, I would like to make some extended comments about this dimension of the formation director's role.

The art of helping others discern vocation

As formation directors, we will probably find no aspect of the work more unattractive than the formulating of our own judgments on the suitability or readiness of candidates. We may even be tempted to take refuge in the saying of Jesus: "Do not judge, and you will not be judged; because the judgments you give are the judgments you will get and the amount you measure out is the amount you will be given" (Mt. 7:1-2). Are we violating this evangelical demand when we make judgments about the suitability or readiness of candidates?

A distinction seems to be in order. It is one thing to make a judgment about the objective morality of certain behavior or the suitability of a person for a specific job or role or the readiness of a person for marriage, priesthood, or the religious life; it is quite another thing to condemn someone because we do not know the precise nature of that person's inner experience or responsibility for present behavior. Jesus forbade the moral condemnation of others; he himself made judgments about right behavior as is evidenced in so much of his teaching. Formation directors have an ecclesial role which involves making the judgment on the appropriateness of behavior, and the suitability or readiness for a walk of life; at the same time, they respect deeply the uniqueness of another's inner experience and they leave the more ultimate judgment about personal responsibility or any culpability to the individual and God.

This distinction is often missed in life. For instance, moral theology which in the recent past focused on the objective judgment about moral behavior sometimes tended to obscure the personal pastoral respect for the individual's unique experience, struggles, and limitations. On the other hand, contemporary moral theology which is attempting to take seriously the experience and difficulties of the people may tend to extend the non-condemnatory pastoral stance to the areas where some objective moral judgments are necessary.

There is an art to making necessary judgments without condemning individual people. This art of discernment involves a humble acceptance of the inspired and proven givens of ecclesial tradition, a profound respect for the uniqueness of the individual's temperament, history and present situation, and a docility to God's mysterious movements of grace. Fundamentally, candidates are called to look at these areas and to make the discerning judgments themselves. They usually have the greatest access to the subjective data needed for such decisions. Moreover, they are the ones who have to live with the decisions that are made. But there is also a two-fold necessity for seeking counsel: they usually do not know the full meaning of the givens of ecclesial tradition and, because of the subtleties of self-deception, they need to test their own appraisal of their personal condition and the movements of God's grace within them. It is for this reason that the Church has consistently taught both the primacy of personal conscience and the need for testing personal conscience with the Church. It is also for this reason that those who present themselves to the Church for public ministry are expected to test their inner experience with those responsible for their formation, both in the internal and external forum.

There are some fundamental factors which make true discernment possible. The first is the genuine desire to do God's will; the second, is the willingness to forego anyone or anything which interferes with responding to God's will. These conditions are necessary both for the spiritual director and the directee.

The concern for discernment is suspect unless there is a true desire to do God's will. Discernment should not become a faddish term to cloak selfish decision-making. Rather, it depends on a burning desire first to know and then to do what God knows to be best. Notice that discovering God's design partly depends on the willingness to fulfill it once it is known, even if there is some initial reluctance experienced. For example, if, as directors, we want too much to see a particular candidate advance, it may keep us from seeing the real obstacles which the candidate is experiencing. Our unwillingness to consider the possibility that God may not be calling this person, blinds us to recognizing that God's will is different from our own. On the other hand, a conscientious willingness to accept whatever is revealed in the directee's life about the authenticity of a call, opens the door to clearer discernment.

The other side of a sincere desire to do God's will is the willingness to give up whatever may stand in the way of fulfilling God's will. It is the willingness that is important. Various obstacles may temporarily limit a response. But if we *want* to ask God's grace and seek out any appropriate human assistance to increase inner freedom, we become more open to recognizing God's will. Thus, if as indicated above, we want a candidate to continue on to the diaconate, priesthood, religious consecration, or another Church ministry too much because of our own needs, we make it almost impossible to help this person discern accurately God's true call. Moreover, it is also possible for us to see nothing but inadequacy and unsuitability in a candidate we do not like. That is why it is important for us to continue to grow in self-knowledge, the desire to be true to God and detachment of spirit.

The same point was made by Jesus in Matthew's account of the Sermon on the Mount. After reporting Jesus' command not to judge, Matthew continued: "Why do you observe the splinter in your brother's eye and never notice the plank in your own? How dare you say to your brother, 'Let me take the splinter out of your eye,' when all the time there is a plank in your own? Hypocrite! Take the plank out of your own eye first, and then you will see clearly enough to take the splinter out of your brother's eye" (Mt.7:3-5). Blindness, due to inappropriate attachments or unfaced problems, can make it impossible to see how God may be at work in a directee. Thus, the inordinate need to "produce" some candidates to justify our work in a time of a dearth of vocations can incline us to overlook some real inadequacies in the candidates. Or the failure to look humbly at our own authority or sexual tensions can lead us to be either unreasonably tolerant or intolerant in these same areas with the candidates. The sincere attachment to God and detachment from whatever poses an obstacle constitute the most reliable basis for true discernment.

Like Solomon of old, we need to offer the prayer: "Grant me Wisdom . . . to help me and to toil with me and teach me what is pleasing to you . . ." (Ws.9:4, 10). The wisdom to work with others in such sacred decisions is a gift from God. It can be refined and developed, but not given to ourselves. It can also be severely hampered by personal moral failure, as happened in the case of Solomon. His attachment to foreign women eventually turned his heart from true worship of Yahweh and impaired his capacity to offer wise counsel or to judge with spiritual insight and justice (1 Kg.11:9).

Thus, in our formation work, we discover that there is a direct correlation between our own growing desire for God and detachment of spirit and our ability to foster these conditions for discernment in others. Our own solicitude for cultivating these attitudes will prompt us to encourage the same dispositions in the candidates.

It may be helpful at this point to draw attention again to some truths developed at greater length in the chapter on "Clarifying Vocation in Life." Discernment of vocation takes place on at least three levels: the inner call to a special path to holiness of life; the call to a specific state of life; finally, the call to a particular occupation within the state of life. We want to focus the attention of the candidates principally on the first. Can the candidates begin to clarify the characteristic ways in which they have experienced God's closeness during their lives? Are there situations, people, events, experiences that have especially moved them and unfolded for them something of the way in which God usually draws them? Is there any message in these? Any thread running through them? Any sense of how God reveals his face to them?

If candidates are able to reflect on this gently and patiently before God, there is going to be a strengthening of the desire for God and his will as well as an increased freedom for the candidates to look at the reasons that brought them into the seminary, novitiate, or training program. The more that sincere attachment to God becomes primary, the more every other consideration will fall into perspective. Those who really discover this can move into much greater freedom about their decision to continue in or to leave a formation program. The desire truly to discover God's will and to do it includes God's will about a state of life. Once this has crystallized, the candidates can look at the experience they are then having in the formation program and compare it to this inner experience of God's special call to holiness of life. Do the particulars of daily life help them to give that inner call flesh? Does the life of priest or deacon or Church minister offer a reasonable expectation for following out this inner call? Or does another walk of life seem to express better this inner call?

It is, then, much more possible to look with equanimity of heart at the various alternatives available. Candidates can project themselves in their imagination into these different possibilities and try to assess how they would correspond to their inner sense of God's way of calling them to himself. Thus, a man may begin to accept that he would make a good husband and a good father, yet also recognize that God seems particularly alive for him as he anticipates helping others, including his married peers, respond to God in their own lives. Although a lay person can do this in some real ways, he realizes that this is more possible with a celibate priestly ministry. A woman in a ministry-training program may begin to sense that the demands of ministry will create a serious strain on her marriage and recognize her prior commitment is to husband and family. She may decide instead on some limited volunteer ministry.

There is no substitute for a growing appreciation of one's own personal salvation history. All have experienced certain very significant people, places, and events which have shaped their way of experiencing God. These factors are going to have a very significant influence. This influence will be mixed, partly good, partly bad. During the period of formation, there is a special value to developing the art of reflecting on the relationship between personal history and the characteristic ways in which a person reacts to current people, events, and possibilities in life. If candidates can begin to distinguish between their wholesome, constructive patterns of behavior and their unhealthy, destructive patterns, they will find themselves in a more graced position to discern their authentic vocational call.

The difference between positive and negative signs

Because of the gospel injunction, "Do not judge" (Mt.7:1), we who are in the formation role may be reluctant to formulate negative judgments. There is a special need for us to foster a climate which is accepting of each person. We image God's personal love, care, and concern. We want to foster an atmosphere in which genuine trust can facilitate personal self-revelation and growth. We seek to be supportive and encouraging particularly for those who have known little or no such affirmation in the past.

But, as indicated above, there is an important distinction between the judgment about suitability or readiness and the condemnation of a person. We do not want to condemn a candidate. We seek, rather, to understand and facilitate growth and conversion. But we do have to decide on suitability and readiness. Suitablity has to do with the basic capacity and gifts for the life; readiness has to do with the appropriate progress in preparation for the step under consideration. Obviously, the question of suitability is the more fundamental issue; the question of readiness presumes suitability and addresses the issue of sufficient progress.

In connection with these judgments, there is a significant difference between a positive and negative sign. Positive signs mean that we see indication that everything else being equal, these persons could make suitable candidates or are ready for the commitment they are about to make. It does not mean that we can tell a candidate, "You have a vocation." We have to be very detached about the decisions the candidates make and encourage them truly to make their decisions before God. We want to support them, no matter how they ultimately interpret the inner call.

On the other hand, we are called upon to deal with negative signs as real obstacles. In an appendix, some of these signs are suggested for the guidance of formation personnel. These signs cannot be dismissed as unimportant. They should be surfaced in conversation with the candidate in accordance with their capacity to face them and the realistic span of time available before commitment. Something of authenticity is lost in the relationship if serious obstacles are ignored until the actual time of deliberation on commitment.

Although the main focus of formation ministry is on fostering the positive response and growth, we are also going to have to help candidates deal realistically with the serious obstacles which stand in the way of ordinary progress. We ought not be so concerned if a candidate has some of the signs which suggest caution. No one is perfect. But we ought to be concerned if the candidate does not seem to be able to do anything about what lies beneath them. Although the Church is not looking for perfect candidates, it is looking for people who can live constructively with their immaturities and weaknesses.

We seek first to provide help for the needy candidate. We may offer our own. If this is insufficient, we can do what seems appropriate to facilitate the possibility of good professional help. In the case of those who are receiving psychological help, we will want to continue to work with them to foster the spiritual dimension of the counseling or therapy.

As the time for the candidate to make either an initial decision or a permanent commitment approaches, then we will have to crystallize our own judgment. Will we raise serious questions about suitability or readiness? If there is a coalescence of a number of serious caution signs, we should have the courage to make the judgment that the inner strength for the oblative love appropriate for candidates in Church ministry is not there. When there is a coalescence of some of these signs, yet there is also considerable evidence of growing self-awareness and some progress and the decision is only for initial commitment, then there is more room for leeway in allowing a candidate to continue to face the issues within the life. If, however, this same person is approaching a final decision and has received significant help with very limited discernible progress, then it seems wise to insist at least on an extended delay, if not on a change into another state of life.

The making of this kind of judgment is indeed very difficult. Probably in no other phase of our ministry will we feel more alone. We are painfully aware of our own limitations, our mixed feelings about the candidate, the significance of the decision for the whole future of this candidate and for the Church. Yet, God has called us to use our human judgment, purified through mortification and enlightened by grace to share in the Church's role of discerning the charismata which he has distributed among his disciples. We do it in fear and trembling. But we do it also in the confidence that God's grace will not be lacking.

God's work

There are many ways in which we who are formation directors can learn from the past and the present to improve the quality of our ministry to those entrusted to our care. One of the aims of this book has been to consider some of these ways.

But ultimately, the ministry of spiritual formation is God's work. In writing to his spiritual offspring in Corinth, Paul said: "I did the planting, Apollos did the watering, but God made things grow" (1 Cor.3:6-7). We cannot lose sight of this saving truth.

Those of us who enter into this sacred ministry are called to humility of heart. Many people tend to idealize spiritual directors. They are supposed to be especially holy because they have been selected for this work of helping others to holiness of life. If we are inclined toward perfectionism in our own life, we may find ourselves enmeshed in the impossible struggle of trying to measure up to all these unreal expectations. We can even be seduced into thinking that the aura in which others may clothe us is real. Or, we may begin to confuse our own growing facility in talking about the spiritual life with genuine personal progress along the spiritual journey. Fortunately, God usually permits enough humbling experience to bring home our weakness.

We need to submit consistently to the truth. We are in the service of life-giving Truth. The truth about God and his creative, redemptive, and glorifying presence has to be central in our life. We are instruments in a ministry which touches realities that far transcend us. Even while we pour ourselves out in service, we must always recognize that it is in contemplative love of the Lord and the quieting of conflicting desires that we are to find both our sustenance and our wisdom. If we can dwell with the love of the Lord, we will sense something of the supra-logic of the ways of divine love in the hearts of men and women, as they strive to respond conscientiously to Christ's inviting and probing question, "What are you looking for?" (Jn. 1:38)

APPENDIX[1]

Toward Identifying the Spiritual Maturity Appropriate for Church Ministry

Formation personnel usually have to make two separate judgments regarding a candidate's acceptance to Church ministry: one judgment is on basic suitability or acceptance to an initial commitment; the second judgment is on readiness to enter into orders, vows, or a long-term commitment to Church ministry.

1. First judgment on suitability (admission to candidacy for deacons and priests or initial commitment for religious or acceptance as a serious candidate in any ministry-training program): the candidate should be on a journey[2] towards growing communion with God, deeper conversion of heart, a more expansive charity, a more mature love for the Church, and a clearer discernment of vocation.[3]

a) Growing communion with God

(1) Positive signs:

(a) A sense of God's closeness and presence in the ordinary events of life
(b) An increasing capacity to spend extended moments in prayer

(2) Signs which suggest caution:

(a) Spiritual stagnation: the candidate may be experiencing more and more difficulties with prayer, sacramental life, a personal rule of life, and little seems to be happening in personal growth in the life of the Spirit.
(b) The signs of self-indulgence: ". . . fornication, gross indecency and sexual irresponsibility; idolatry and sorcery; feuds and wrangling, jealousy, bad temper and quarrels; disagreements, factions, envy, drunkenness, orgies, and similar things" (Gal.5:19-20).

[1]The author presented a preliminary draft of the material contained in this appendix at the New Orleans meeting of the National Catholic Education Association, April 1973 (cf. *Seminary Newsletter Supplement*).
[2]The words "on a journey" suggest the need to be on a road with at least a beginning awareness and some recognizable progress in each of these areas.
[3]The reader is encouraged to confer pages 133-134 for a suggested approach to the use of the criteria listed in this Appendix.

b. Deeper conversion of heart:

(1) Positive signs:

    (a) A growing self-knowledge and self-acceptance
    (b) Acknowledgement of need to be redeemed
    (c) Sincere desire to become a disciple of Jesus Christ
    (d) Openness and willingness to be taught

(2) Signs which suggest caution:

    (a) No real inner direction in life: external performance may be erratic as reflected in attendance patterns, work patterns, and the handling of responsibilities.
    (b) Inability to take some personal responsibility for what goes wrong in life: a tendency to blame others and a refusal to accept any correction for even serious shortcomings.

c. Expanding the life of charity:

(1) Positive signs: patience, kindness, humility, gentleness, unselfishness, forgiveness, compassion, tolerance, trust, hope, endurance (cf. 1 Cor.13:4-6).

(2) Signs which suggest caution:

    (a) An obsessive need for friendship: a person's whole life seems to revolve around envy, jealousy, and depression because of the great craving for friendship.
    (b) An excessive and consistent withdrawal from others: a person may be shy, obedient, and cooperative, but unable to sustain ordinary intimacy in human relationships.
    (c) On-going overt sexual behavior: heterosexual, homosexual, auto-erotic genital activity.
    (d) Excessive hostility with no discernible self-insight: anger projected on other people or institutions with no beginning realization of the internal dimensions to the hostility.
    (e) Refusal or inability to sustain a relationship with any spiritual director: this may mean serious problems in handling intimacy, or anger, or trust in others.

d. Maturing love for the Church

(1) Positive signs:

    (a) Ability to see the Church as embodying Christ's continued presence on earth: human and divine; sinful and holy.
    (b) Ability to see the Church, even with all its shortcomings and sinfulness, as offering authentic teaching, worship in spirit and in truth, and a particular presence of God in the world.

(2) Signs which suggest caution:

(a) Incessant hypercriticism of the Church
(b) Tendency to want to create entirely new ways of worshipping God, expounding faith doctrine or being pastorally present to people.
(c) Extremely rigid adherence to past patterns of worship, doctrinal expression, or pastoral practice with little or no tolerance for appropriate adaptation or for the imperfect approaches of others.
(d) Excessive reluctance to accept hardships and suffering in the exercise of ministry.

e. Clearer discernment of vocation

(1) Positive signs:

(a) A sense of the interior call to holiness whatever the state of life
(b) An interior attraction to a state of life, tested by the Church
(c) An appreciation for Church ministry which involves a voluntary renunciation of other attractive alternatives.

(2) Signs which suggest caution:

(a) No interior attraction to holiness of life
(b) No adequate exposure to other alternatives in life, perhaps coupled with a vague fear of pursuing them
(c) An inadequate emotional or social maturation
(d) Excessive naivete about life in the world

2. Second judgment on readiness (major orders for deacon or priest or final vows for religious or missioning of lay persons): the candidate is ready to serve the Church because of a consecration of sexual love, detachment in life, a willingness to enter into a collaboration, yet subordinate relationship with sacramental authority, a real sharing in ecclesial prayer and a genuine pastoral charity.

a. Consecration of sexual love

(1) Positive signs:

(a) Interior involvement either in a permanent celibate or marital love
(b) Interior attraction to intimacy with God undergirding all human love
(c) Basic happiness in celibacy or marriage
(d) Modesty in dress, manner, words.

(2) Signs which suggest caution:

(a) Merely external involvement in celibacy or marriage
(b) Unhappiness in celibacy or marriage
(c) Preoccupation with genital sexual impulses and inability to handle

them except with great uneasiness and discomfort.
(d) Inability to renounce inappropriate relationships
(e) Excessive preoccupation with winning the admiration of young attractive peers.

b. Detachment in life

(1) Positive signs:

(a) A willingness to embrace a style of life that involves some detachment from worldly comforts
(b) A tangible concern for the poor

(2) Signs which suggest caution:

(a) Disproportionate expenditures of money on luxuries for self
(b) Attitude that Church ought to supply every want and need in return for service
(c) Insensitivity to social issues and especially the plight of the poor.

c. Willingness to accept a collaborative, but subordinate role with sacramental authority

(1) Positive signs: a willingness to accept that the bishop of a diocese is the one who authenticates any share in the ministry of the word and sacrament and who gives a specific pastoral mission.

(2) Signs which suggest caution:

(a) An overly submissive attitude toward authority (compliance in a very rigid and external way)
(b) An overly rebellious attitude toward authority (inability to accept role of sacramental authority)

d. Sharing in ecclesial prayer

(1) Positive signs:

(a) Desire to become a truly prayerful Christian
(b) Willingness to be nourished by Scripture and spiritual tradition
(c) Acceptance of role of praying with and for the people

(2) Signs which suggest caution:

(a) Unwillingness to accept any ecclesial prayer
(b) Inclination to construct public prayer principally from secular sources
(c) Failure to appreciate the significance of becoming pray-ers for the people.

A Practical Guide To Spiritual Formation

e. Genuine pastoral charity

(1) Positive signs:

    (a) A capacity to reach out in genuine care for others
    (b) A capacity to welcome others into life
    (c) Willingness to accept hardship in service to others
    (d) Awareness of transcendent origin of pastoral love

(2) Signs which suggest caution:

    (a) Excessive dependence on acceptance by others: tendency to try to manipulate positive response and to become depressed when acceptance wears thin.
    (b) Excessive self-enclosure: tendency to keep removed from meaningful contact with others
    (c) Unwillingness to suffer in service to others
    (d) Tendency to reduce pastoral love to merely secular caring for others.

Revenue earned by the author through the sale of this book will be used for the formation of candidates seeking to prepare for Church ministry.